the new coloring book

I0472686

\EVERYBODY HAS a MONSTER iNSIDE!

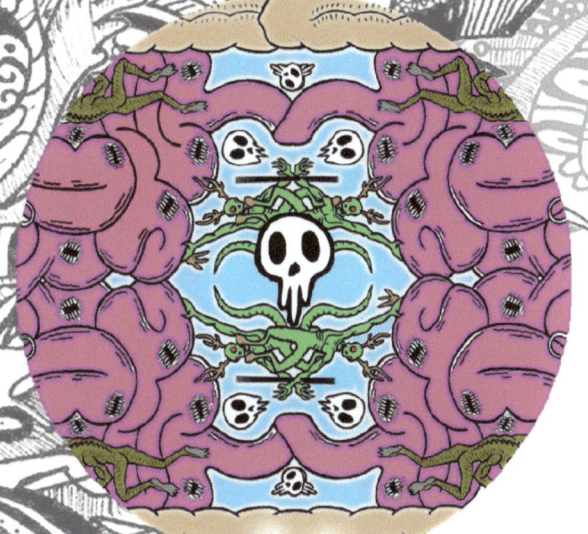

an original by

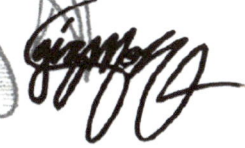

A GIZMOH'S ORIGINAL COLORING BOOK

Title
\EVERYBODY HAS A MONSTER INSIDE

All draws and book design © André Ferreira (Gizmoh) 2015

First Edition
Published in January 2016
Copyright © DEP635859752872319206
All rights reserved
ISBN-10: 1523254947
ISBN-13: 978-1523254941

Printed in Lisbon, Portugal

Available online @
http://gizmohone.webs.com/
http://www.amazon.co.uk/
http://www.amazon.com/

For more about Gizmoh's works, take a look at
http://gizmoh.webs.com/
https://soundcloud.com/gizmoh-1
http://death-above-us.myshopify.com/

Keep in touch
www.facebook.com/Gizmohone/
gizmohofficial@gmail.com

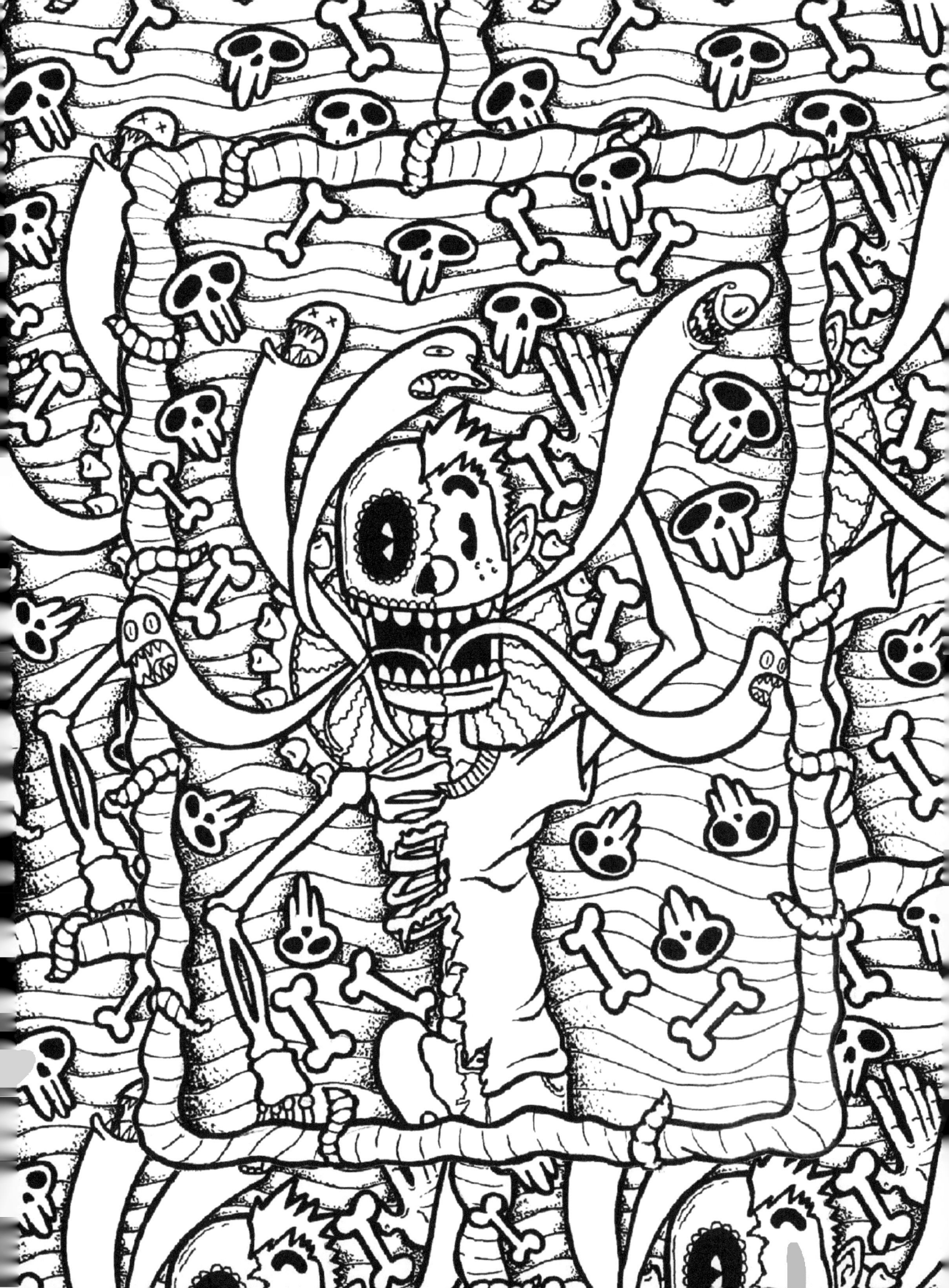

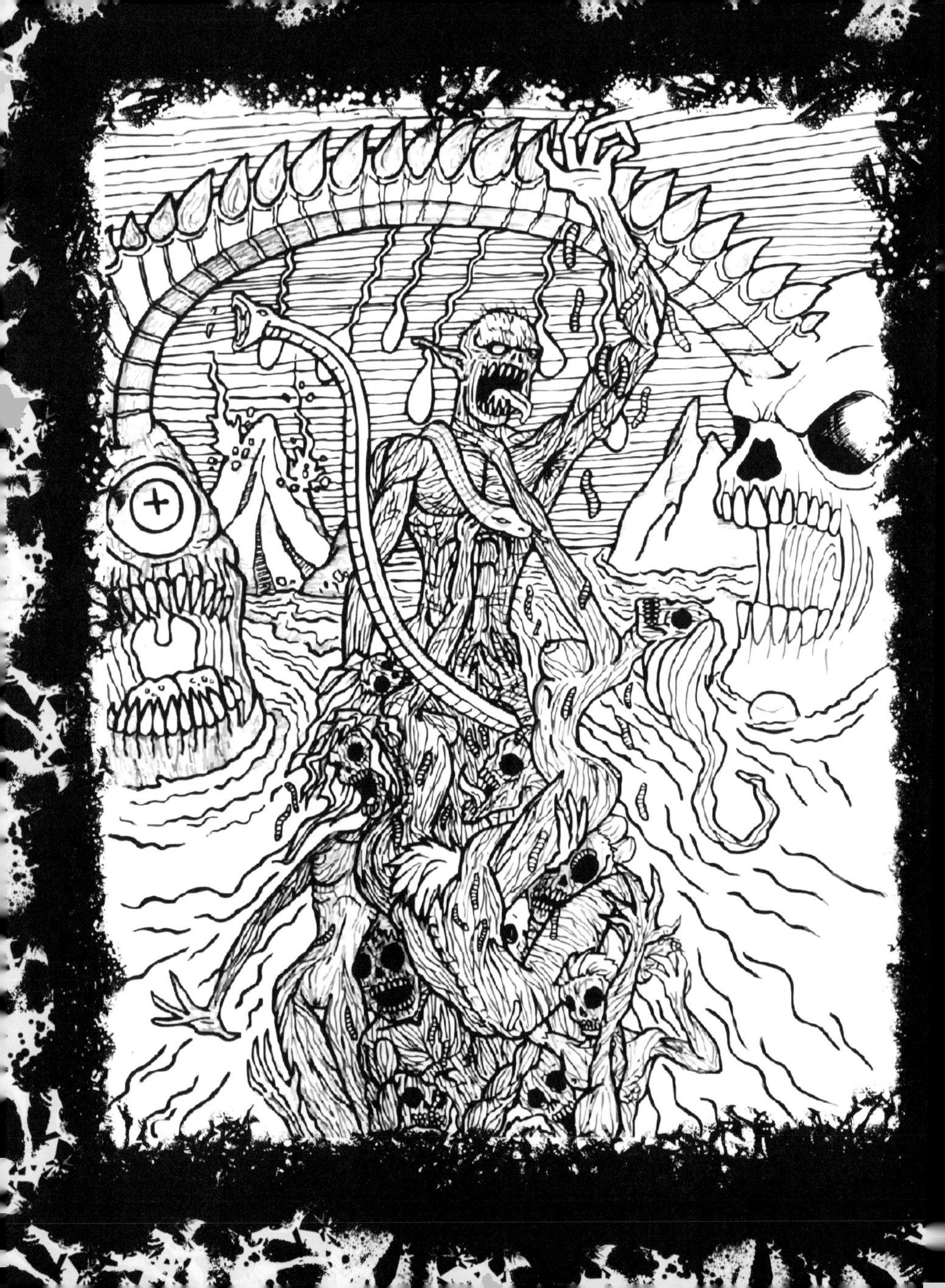

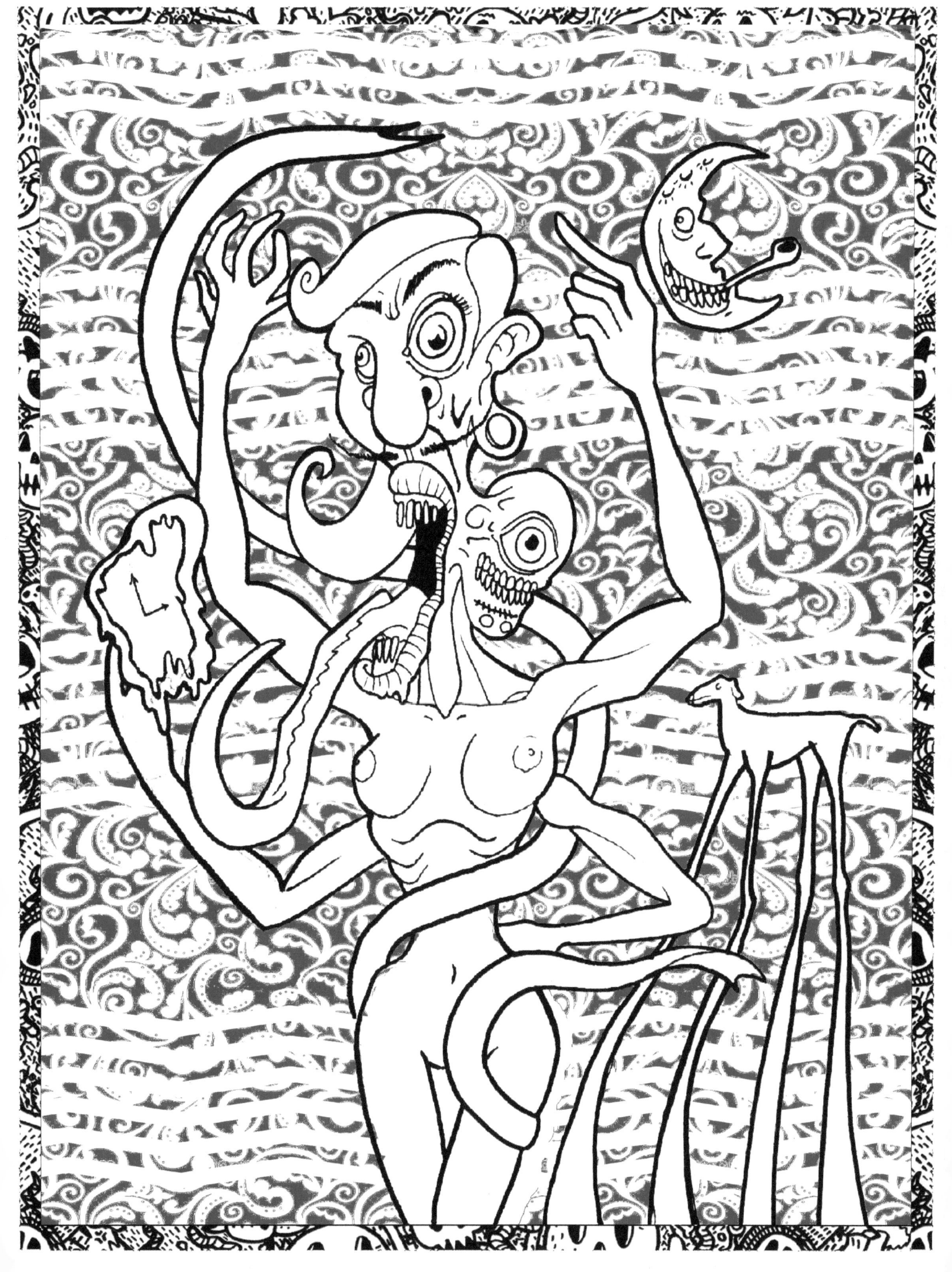

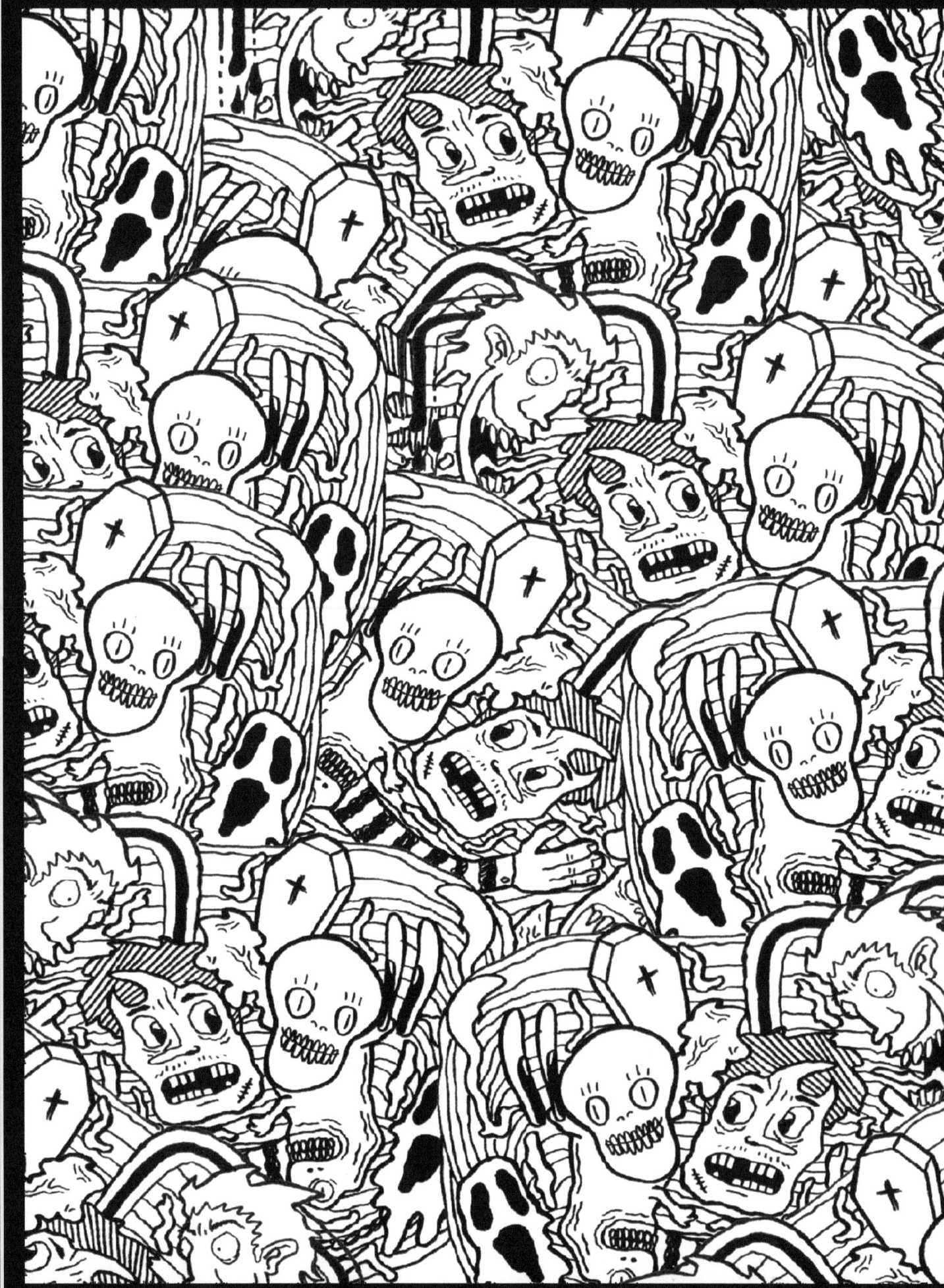

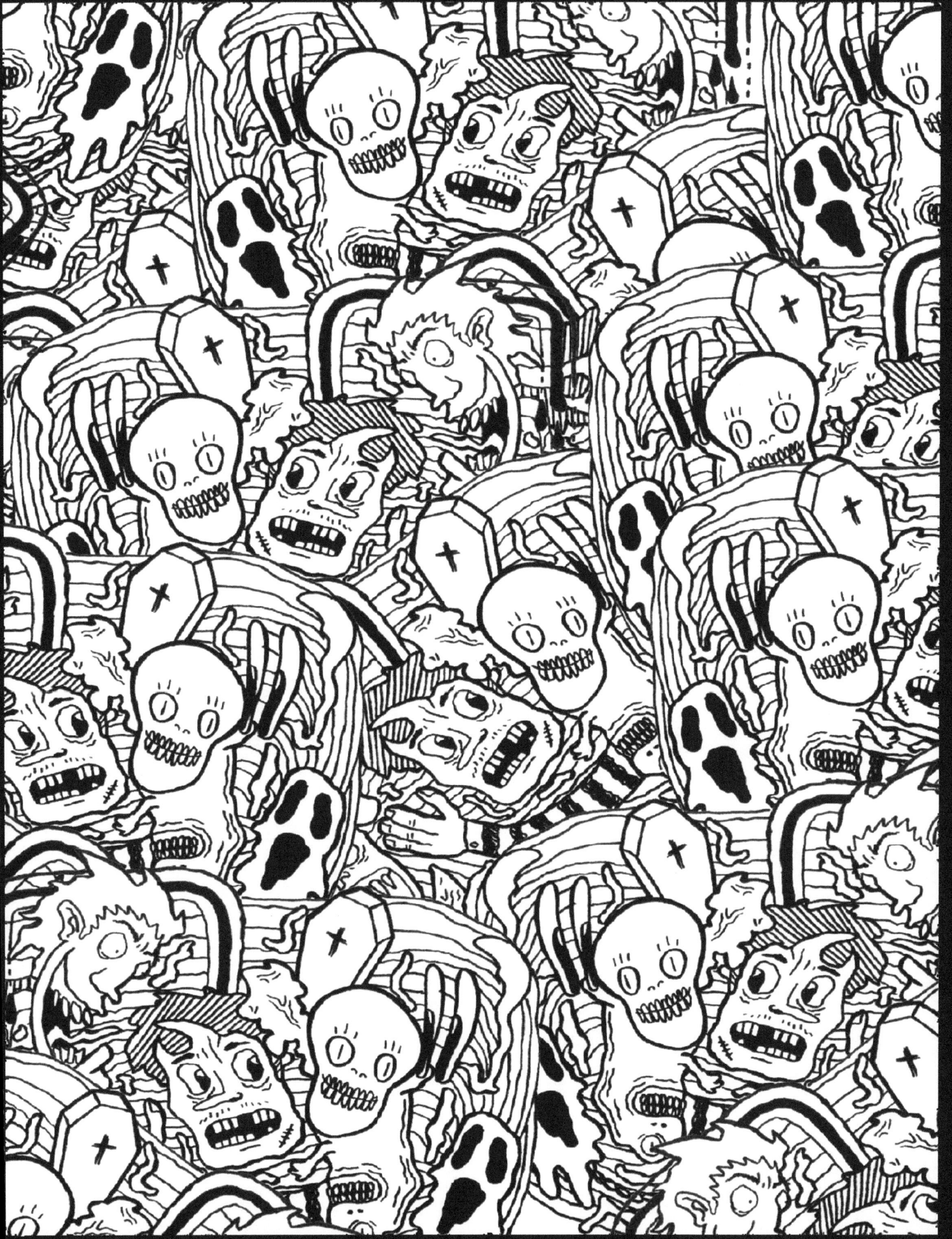

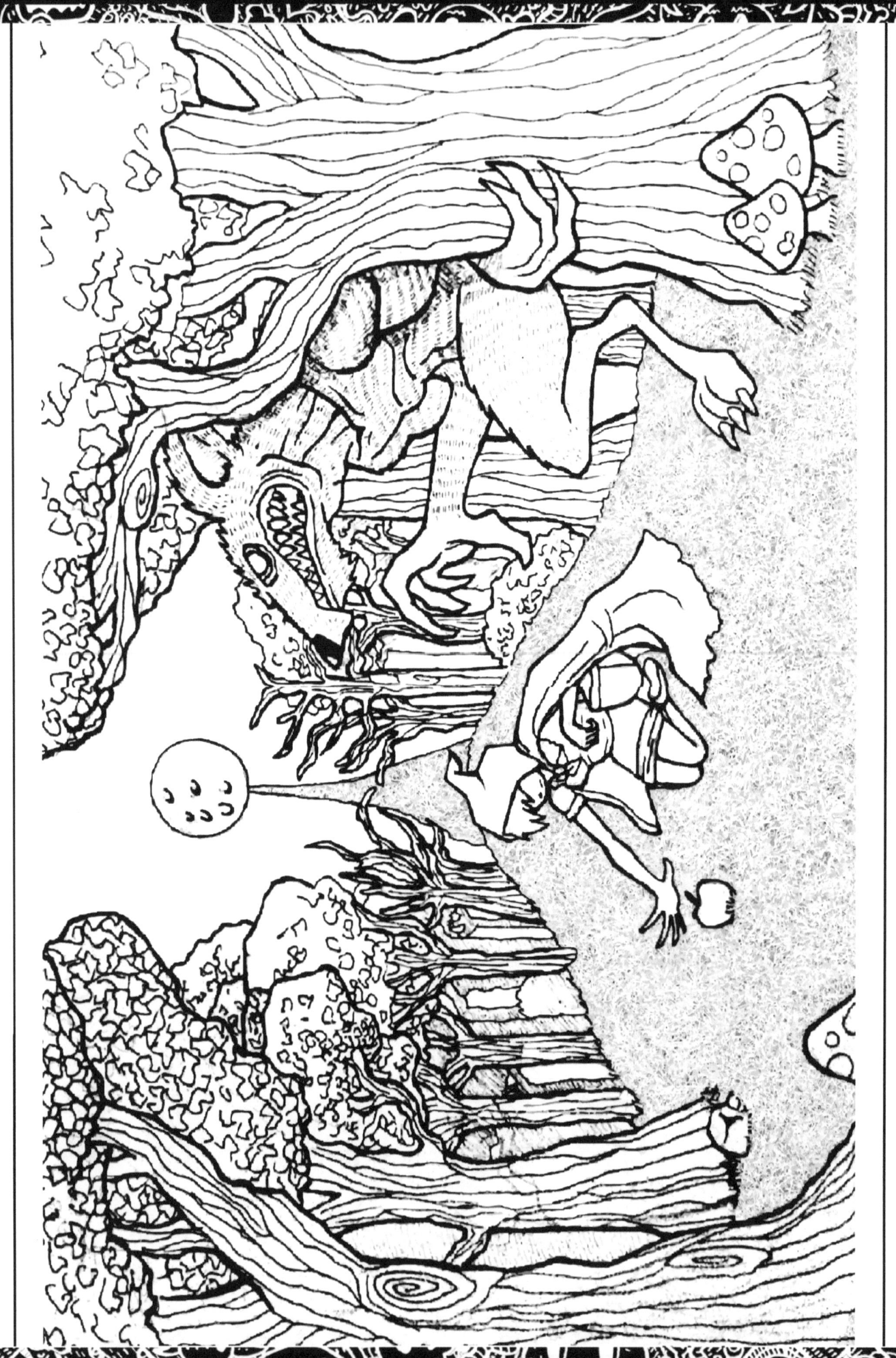

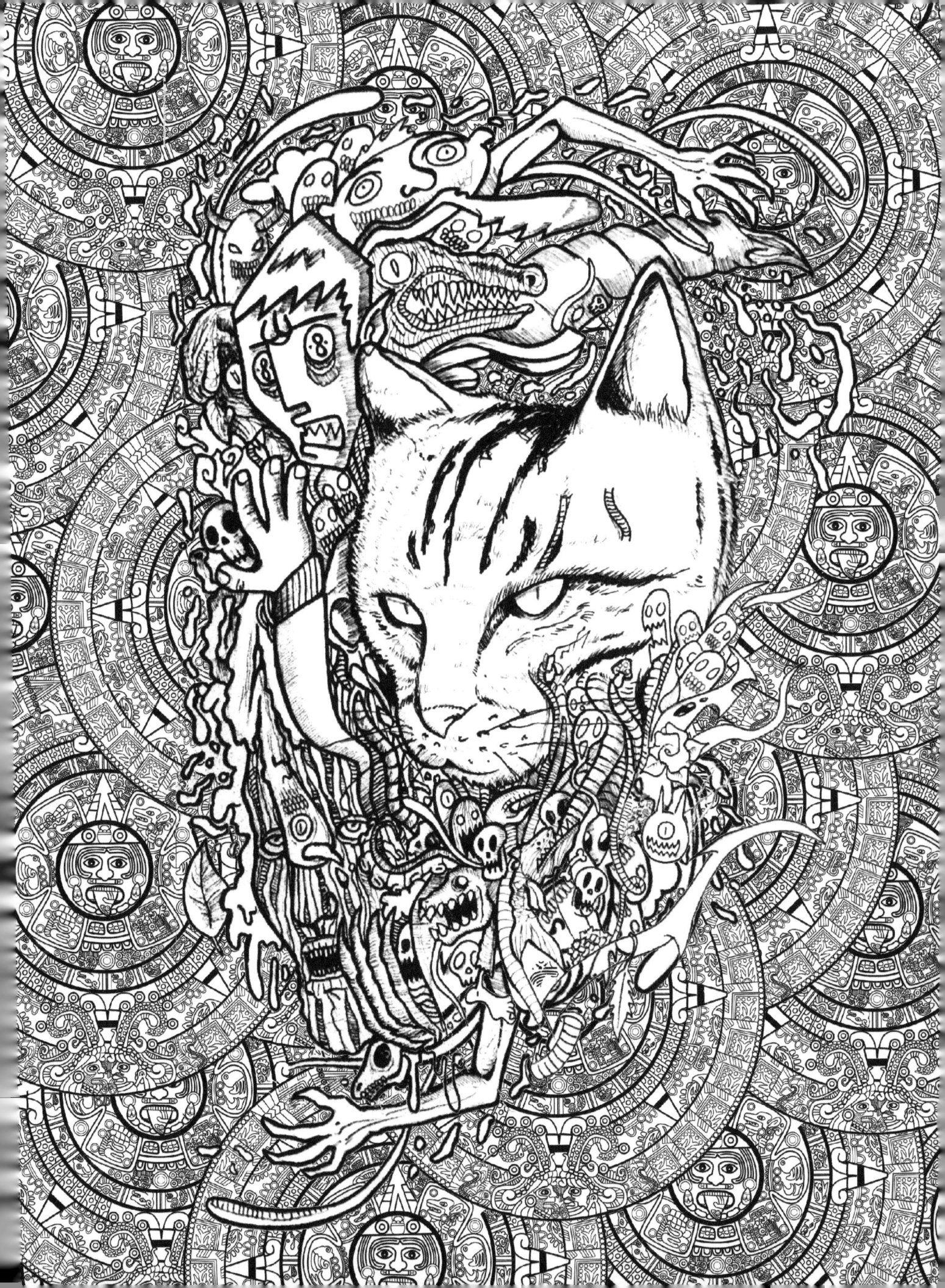

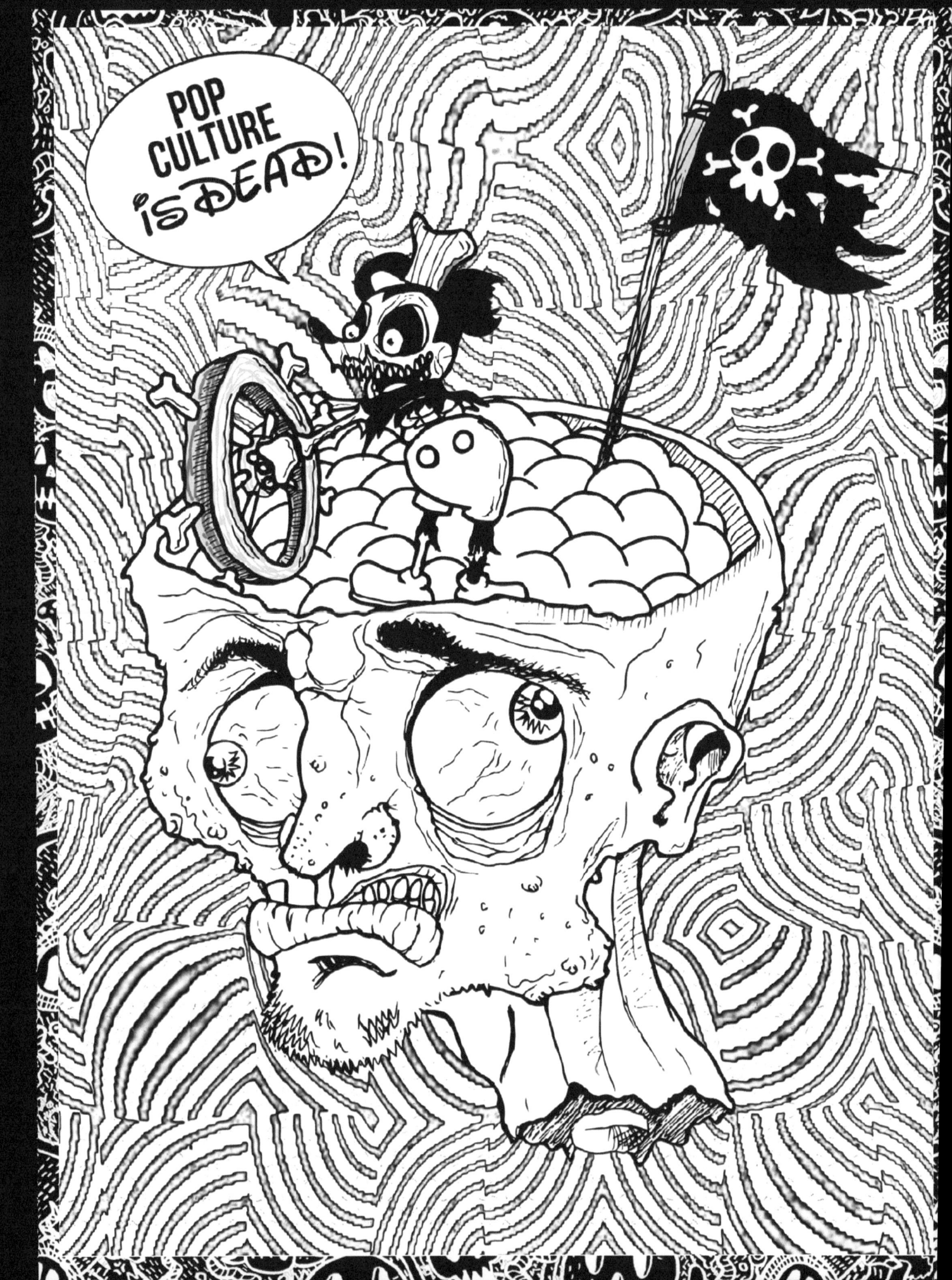

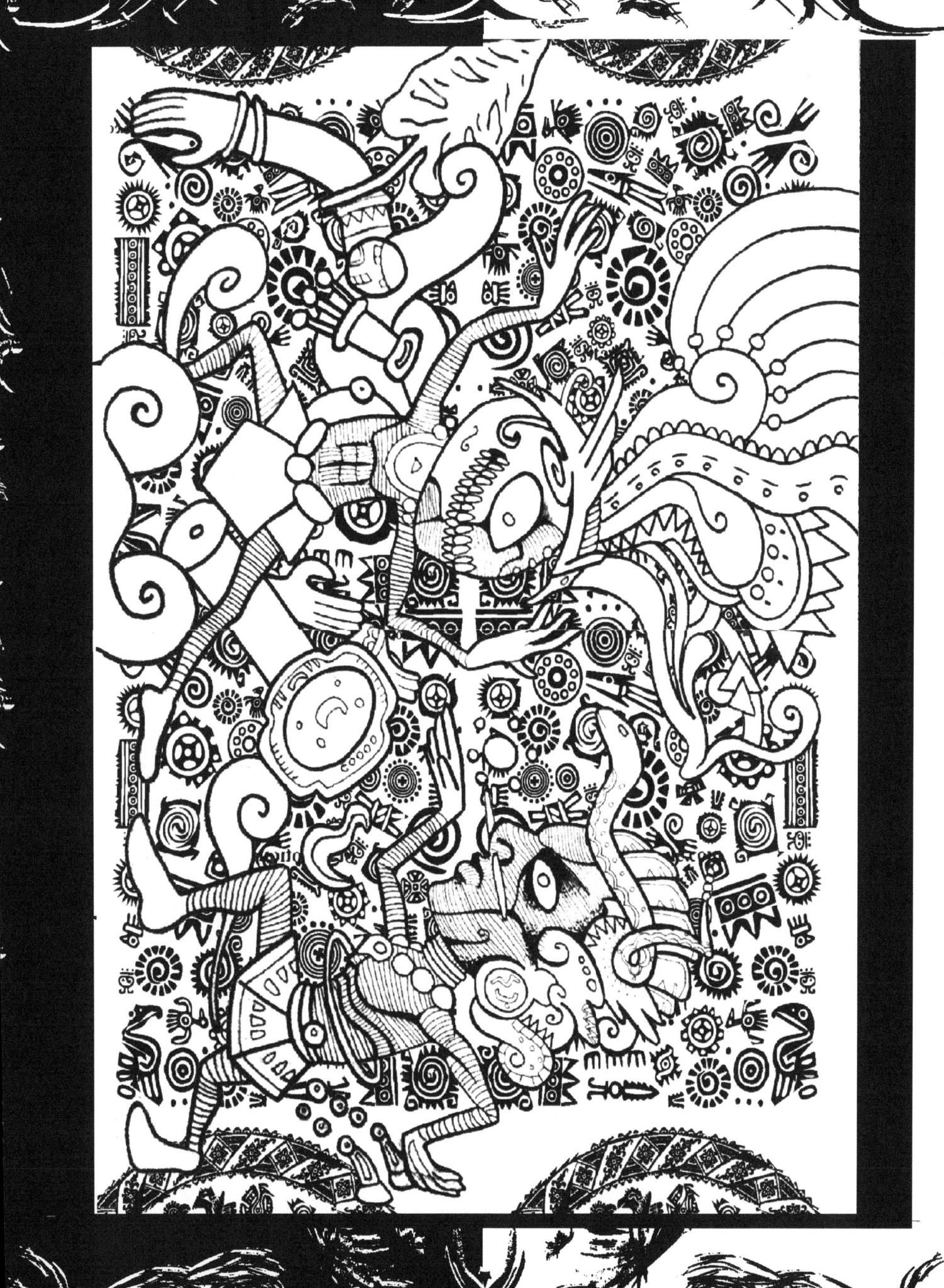

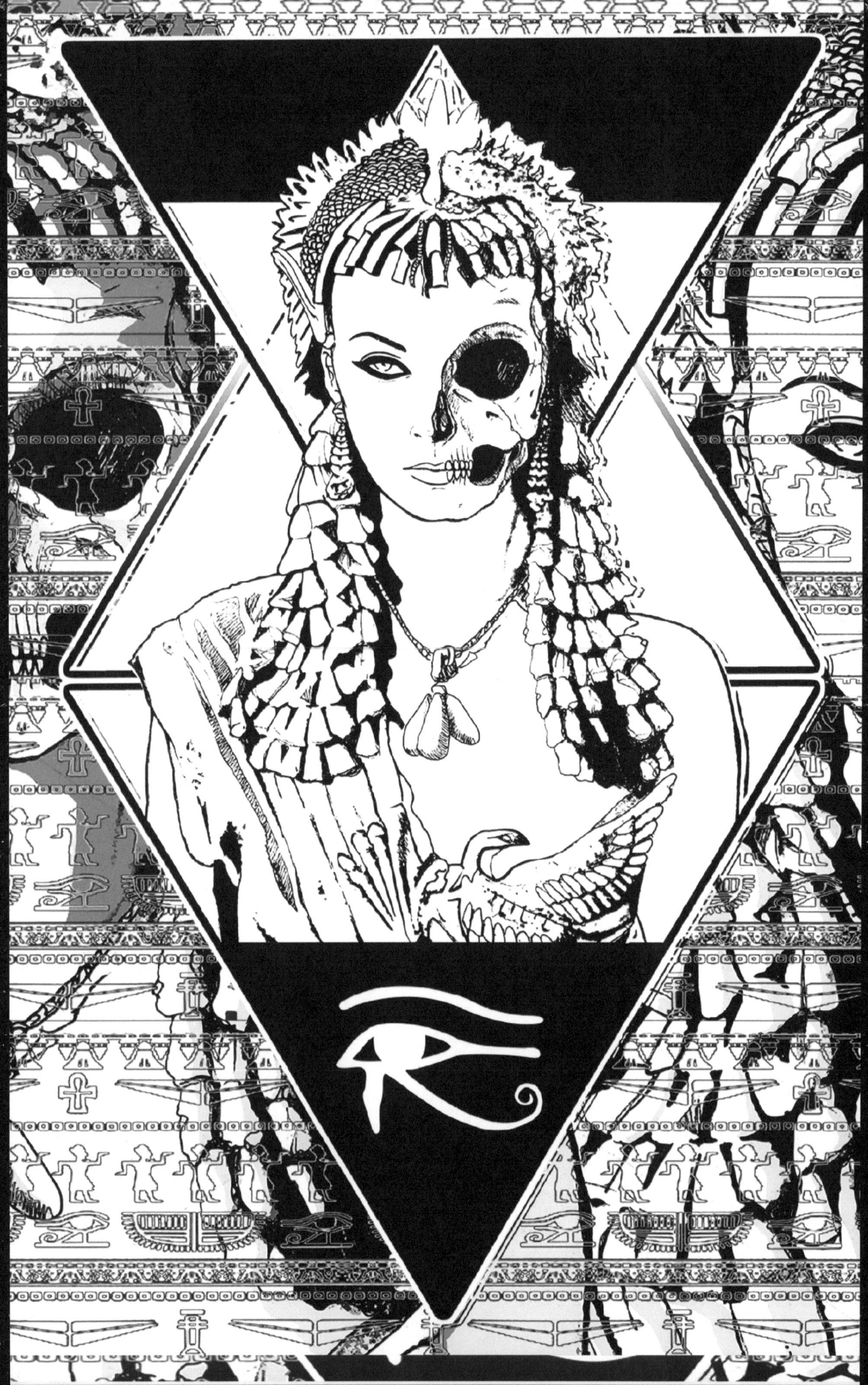

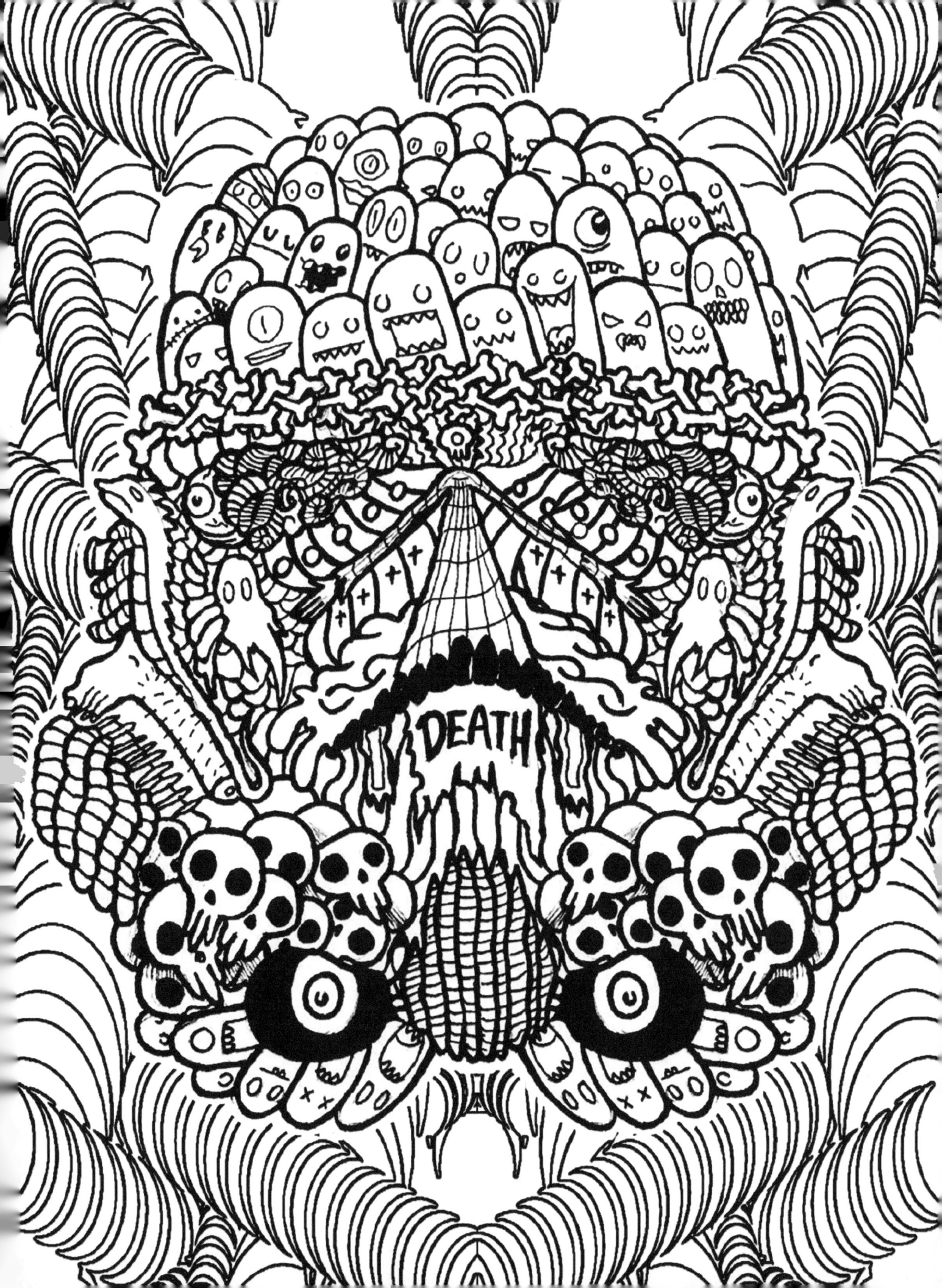

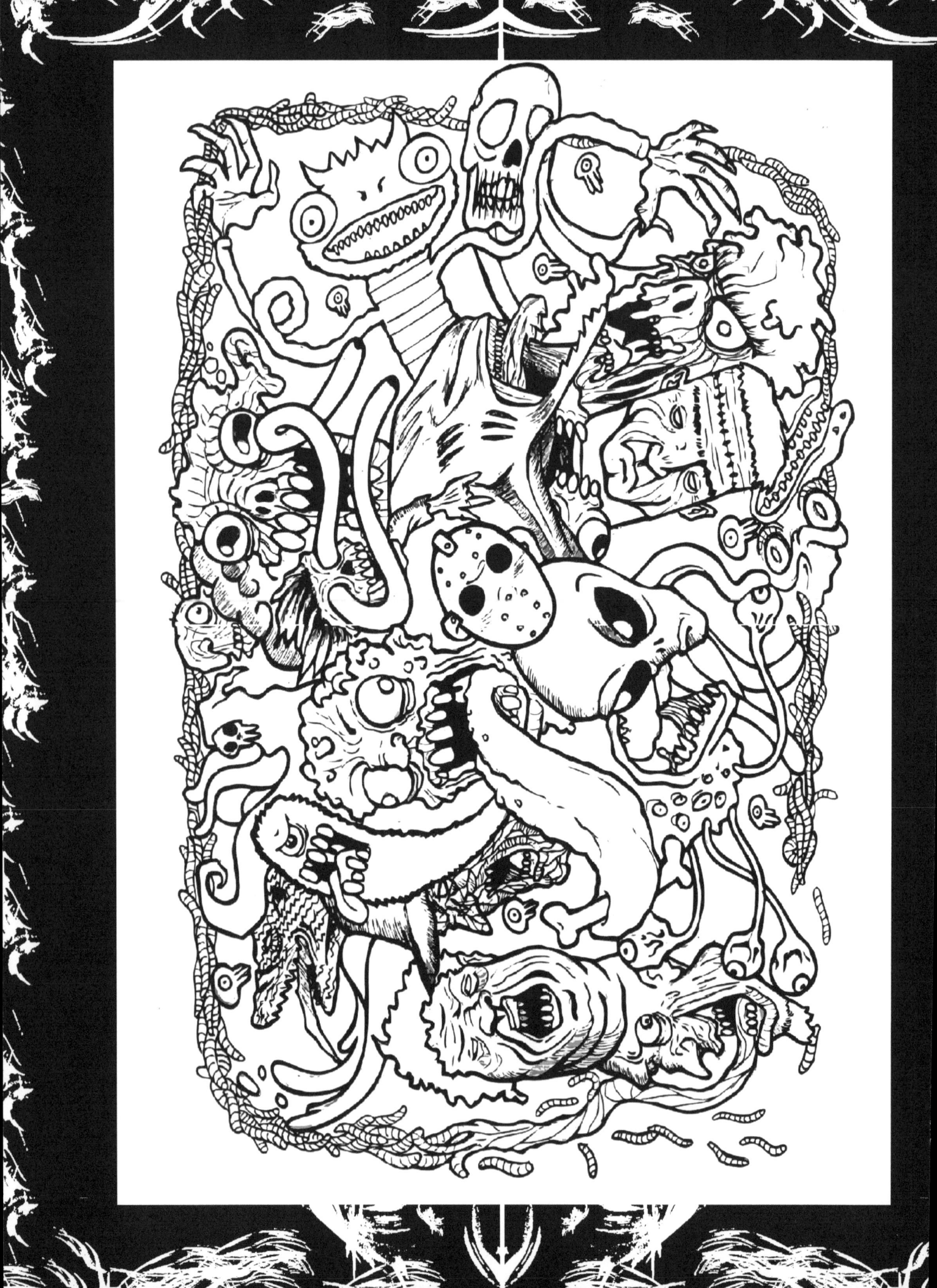

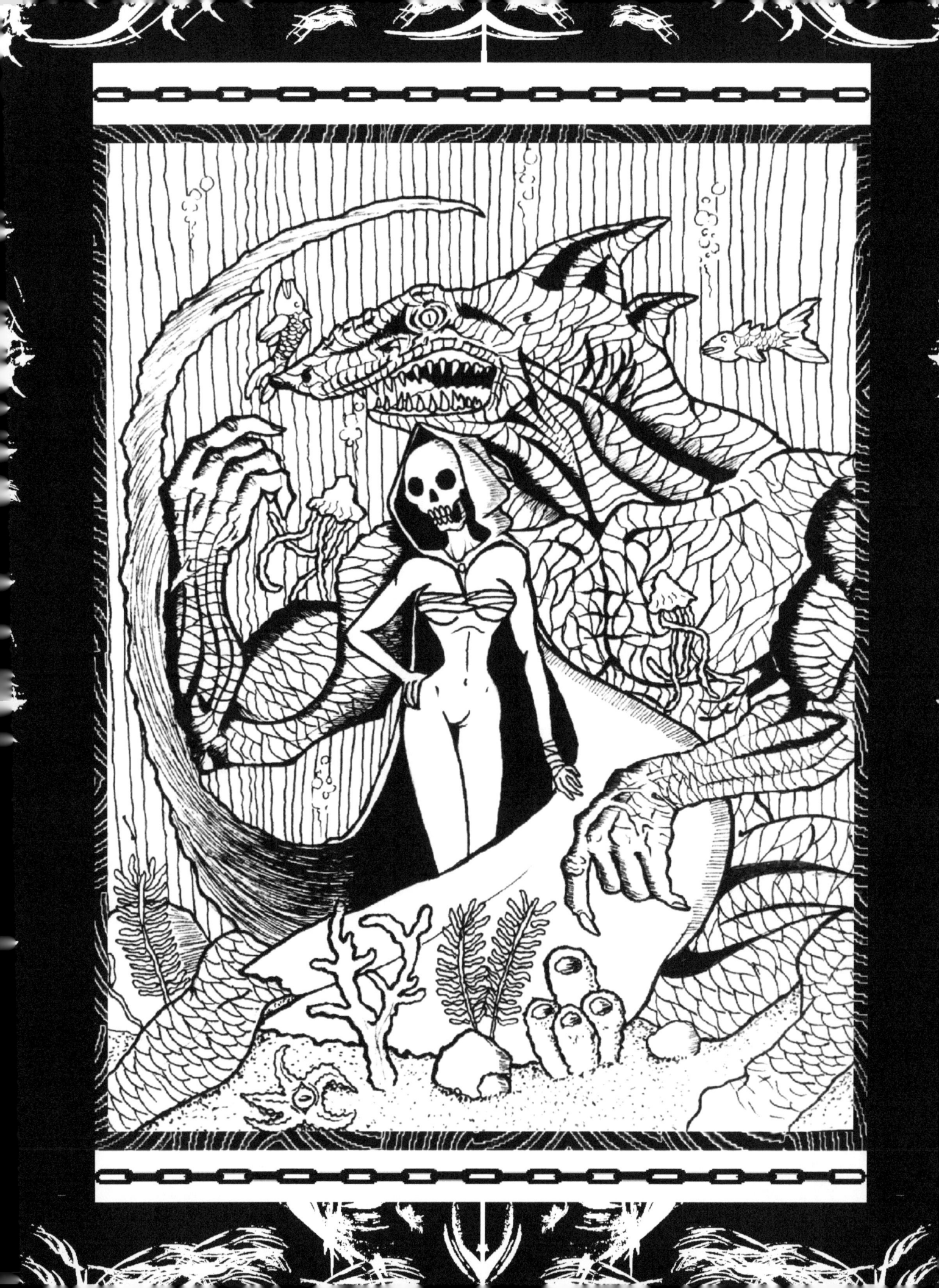

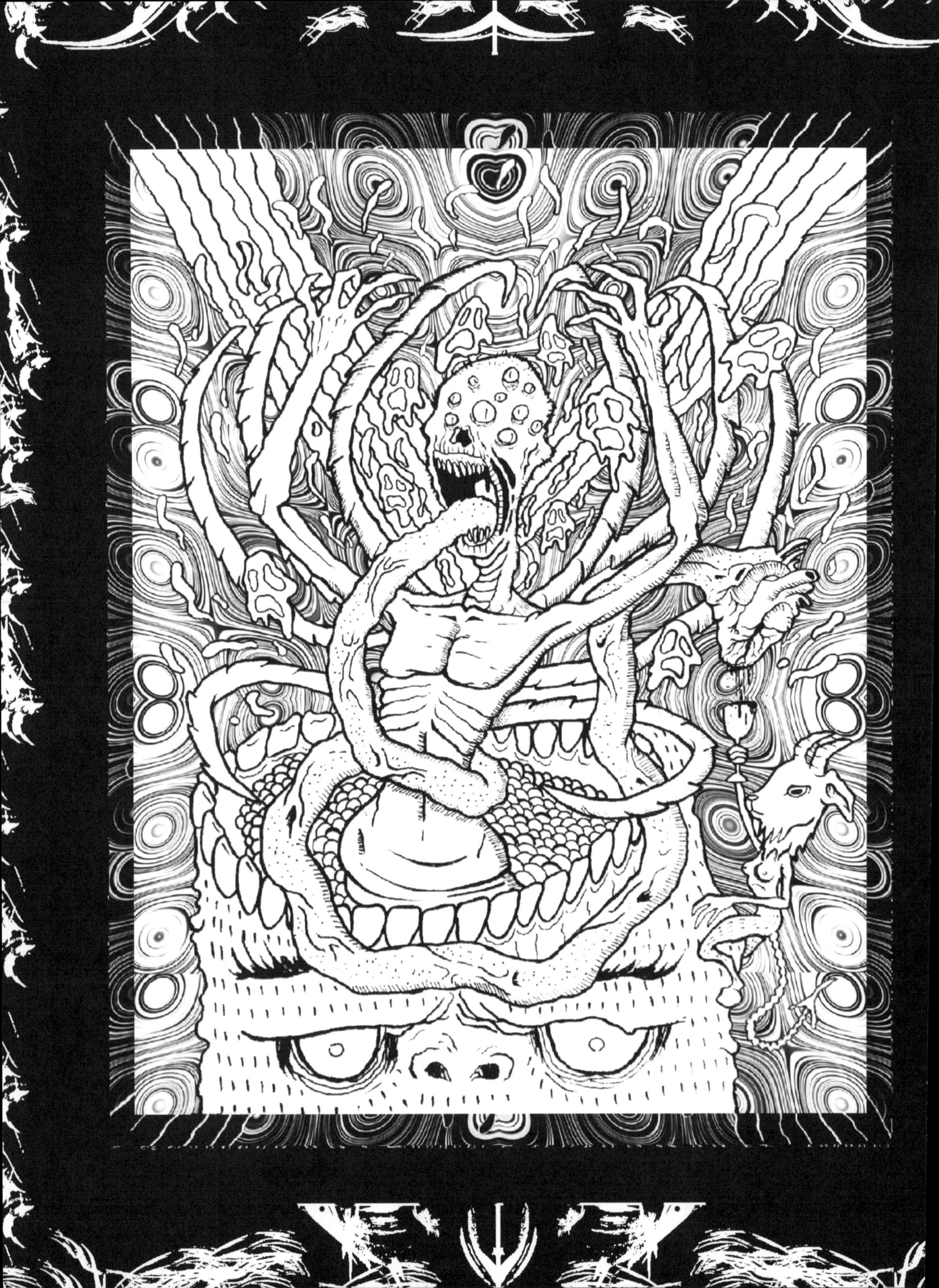

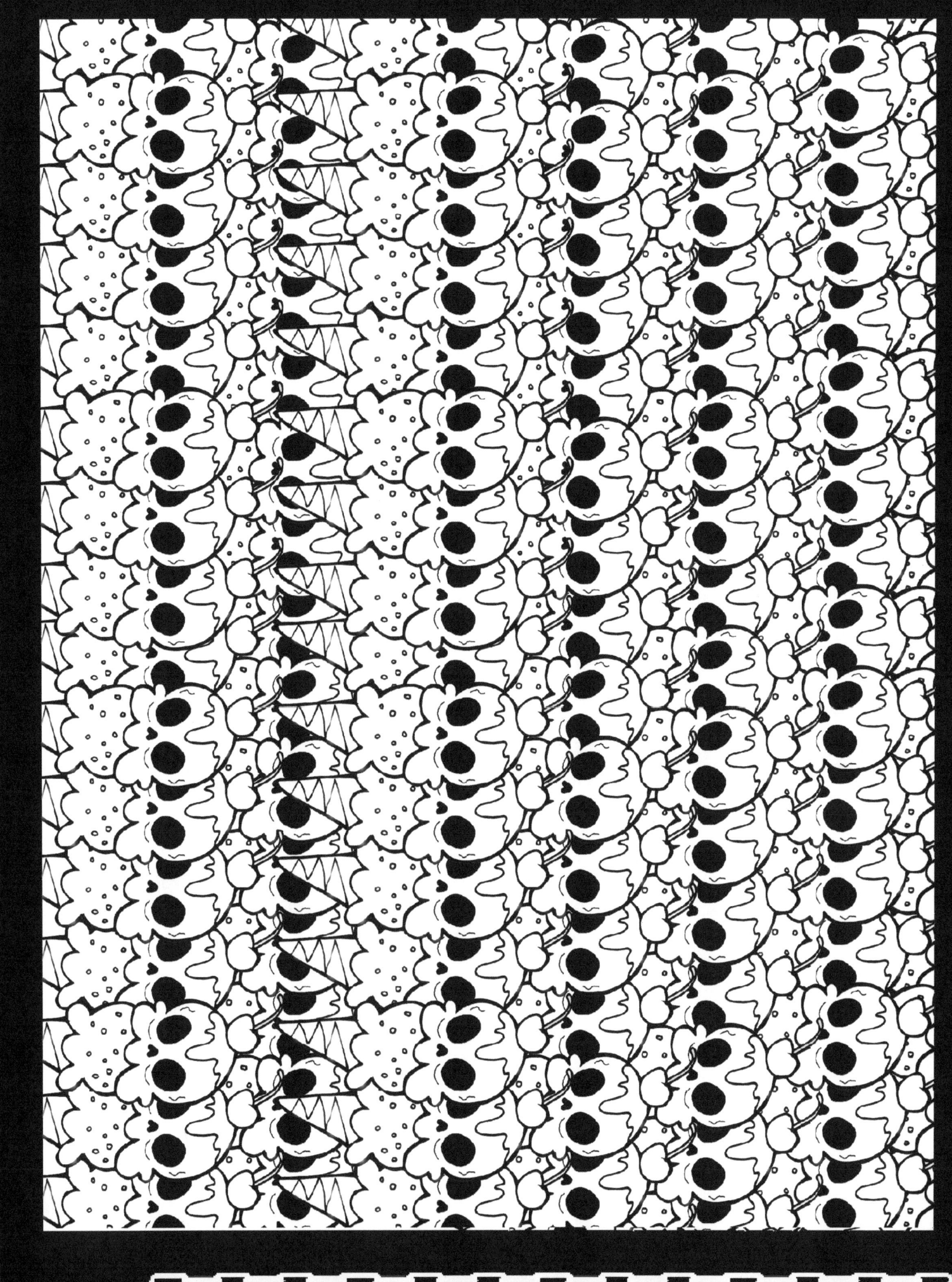

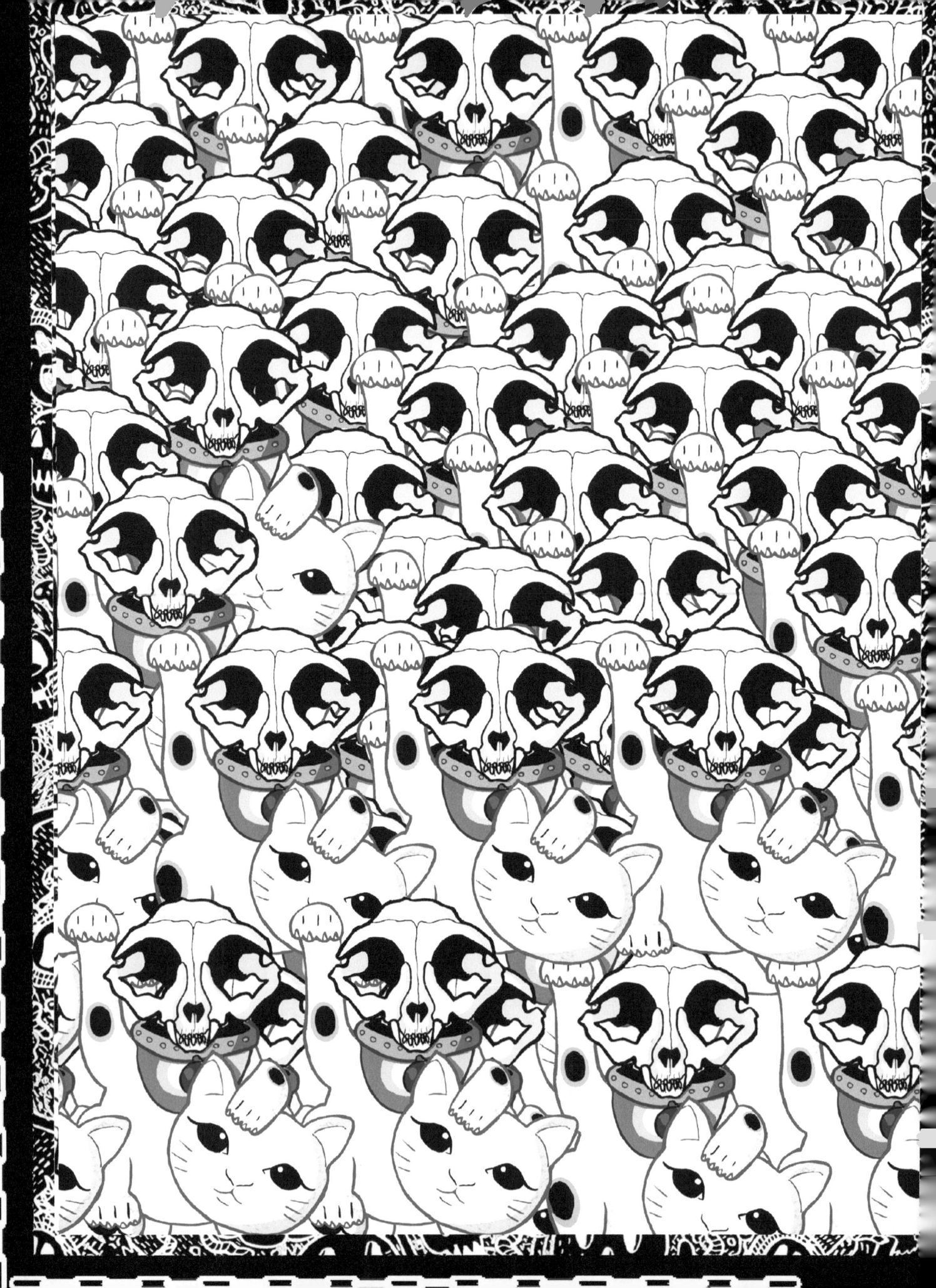

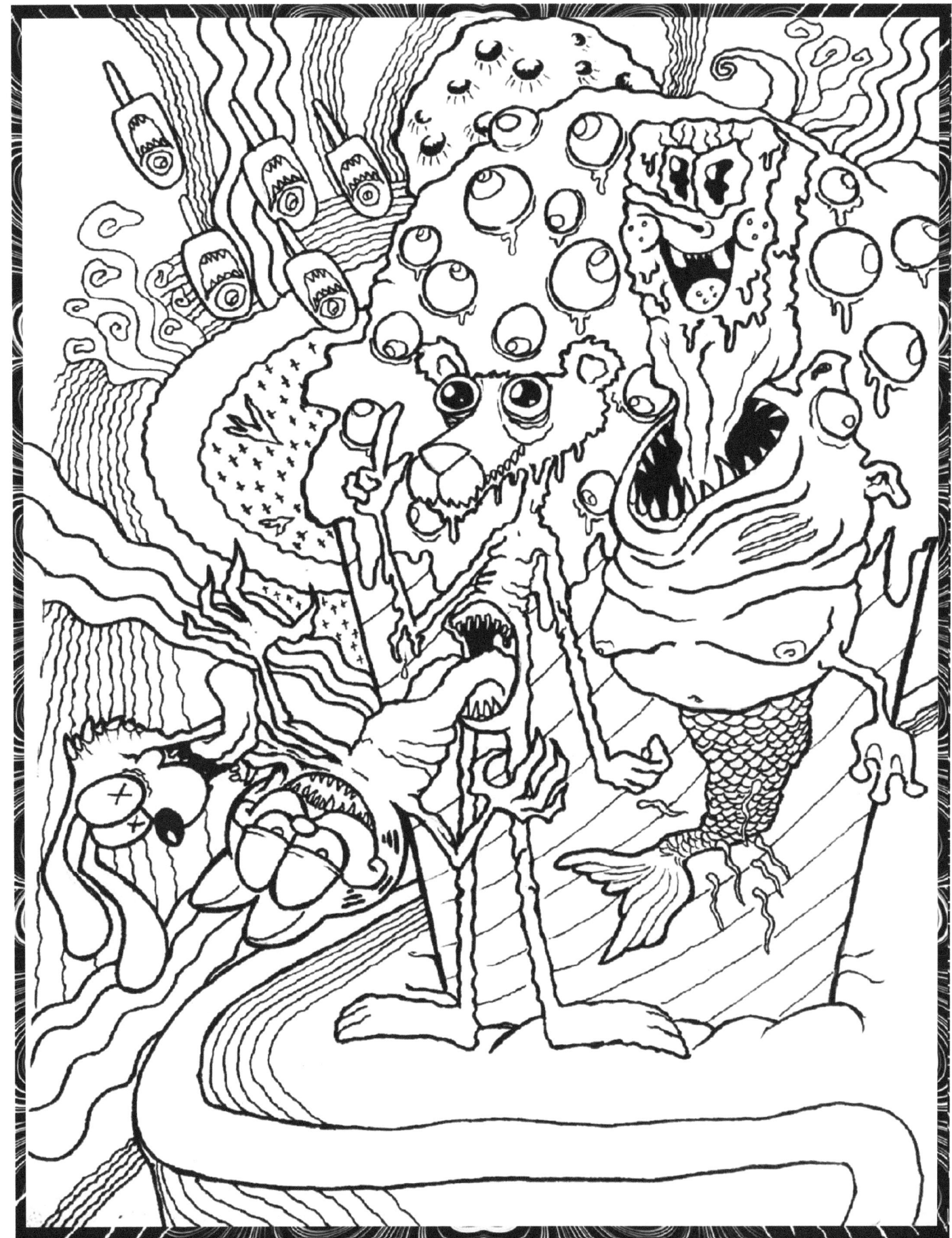

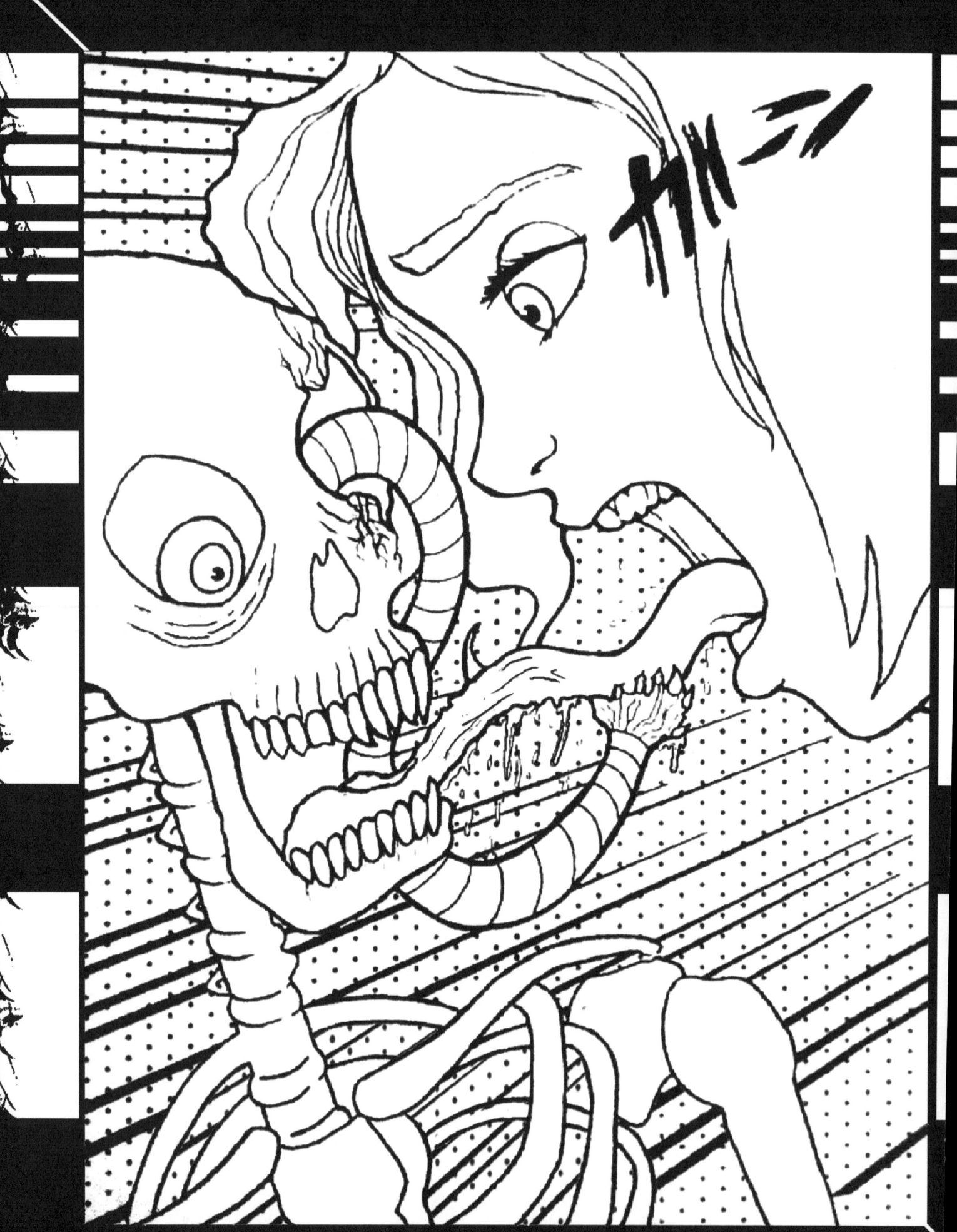

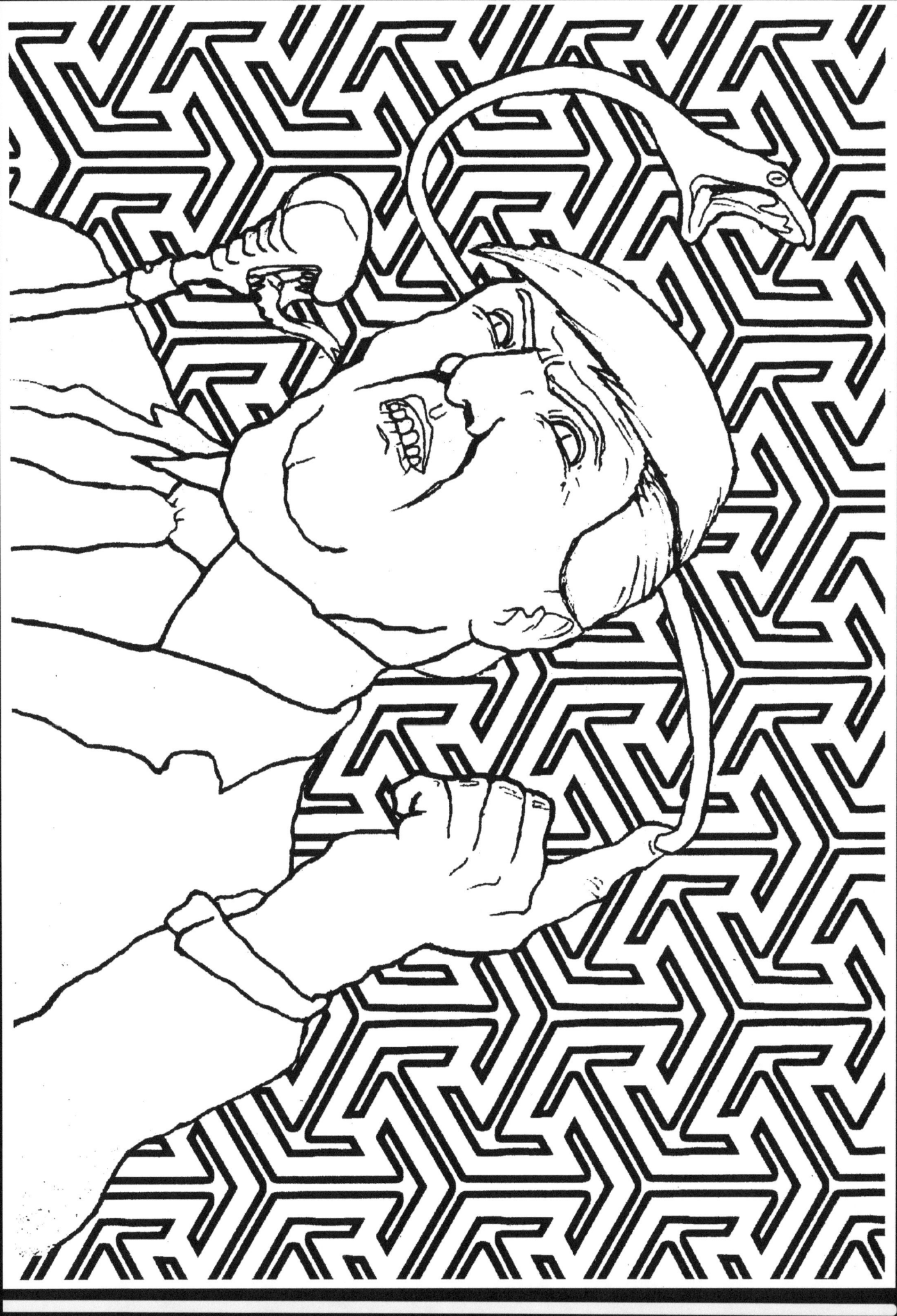

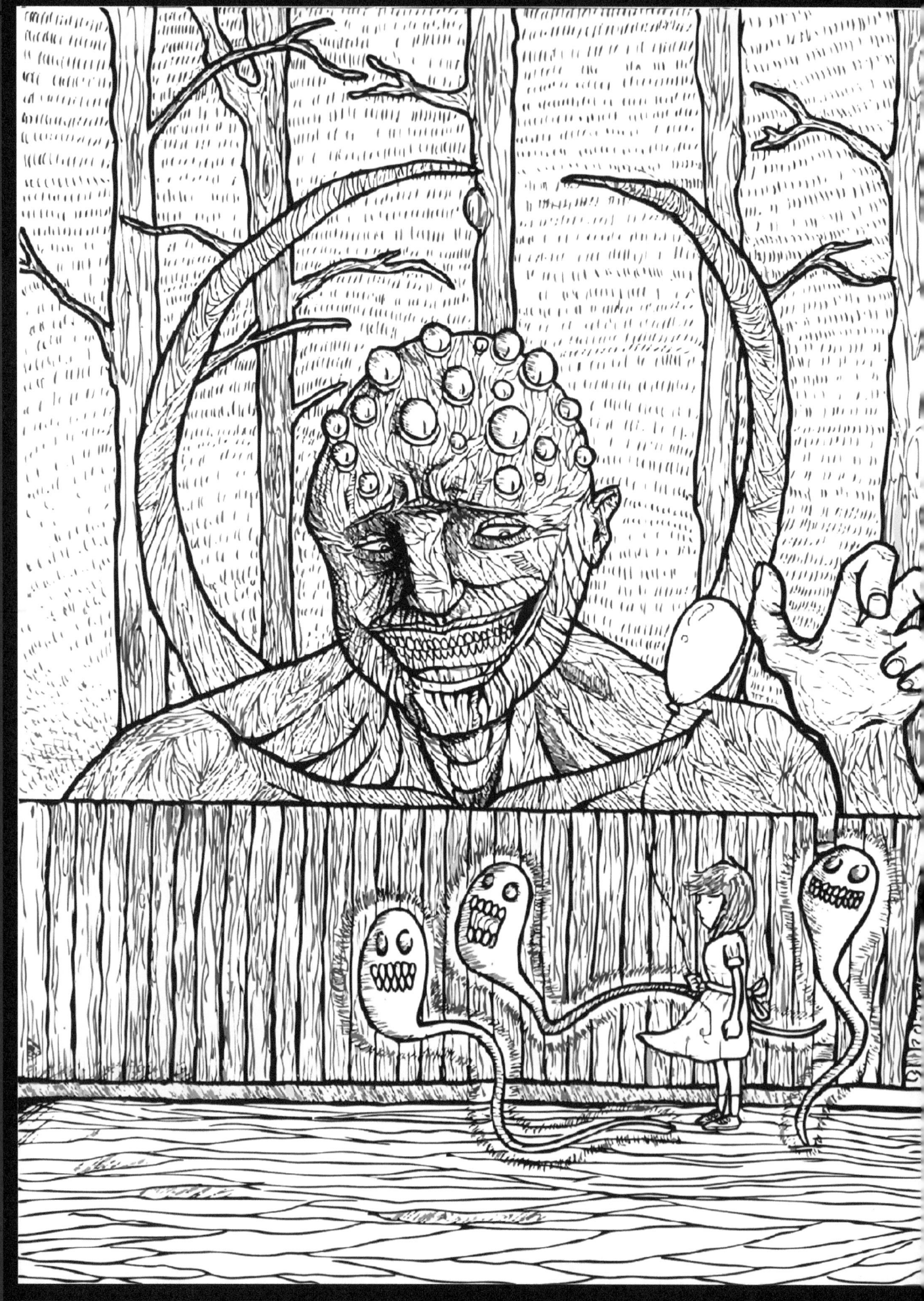

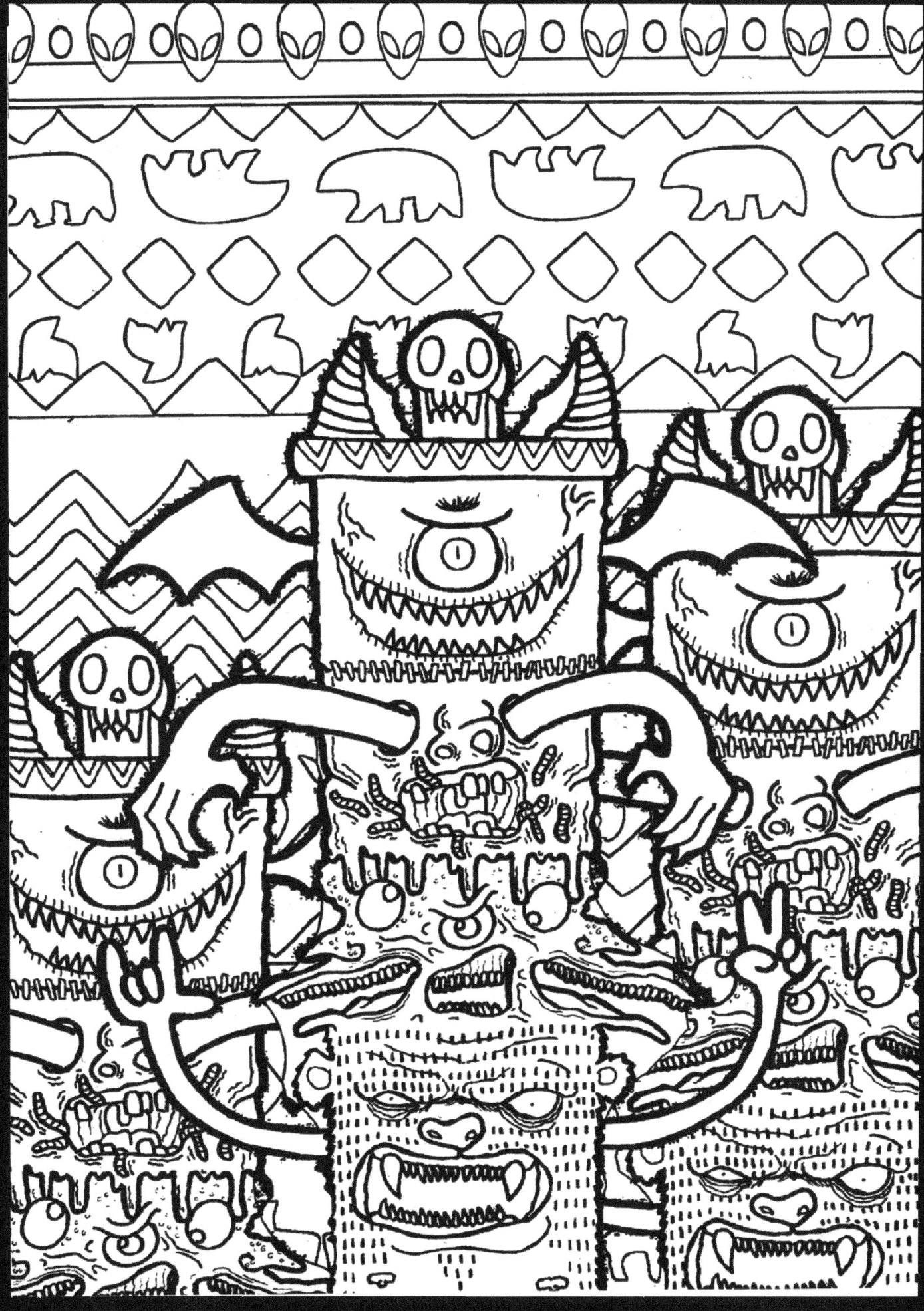

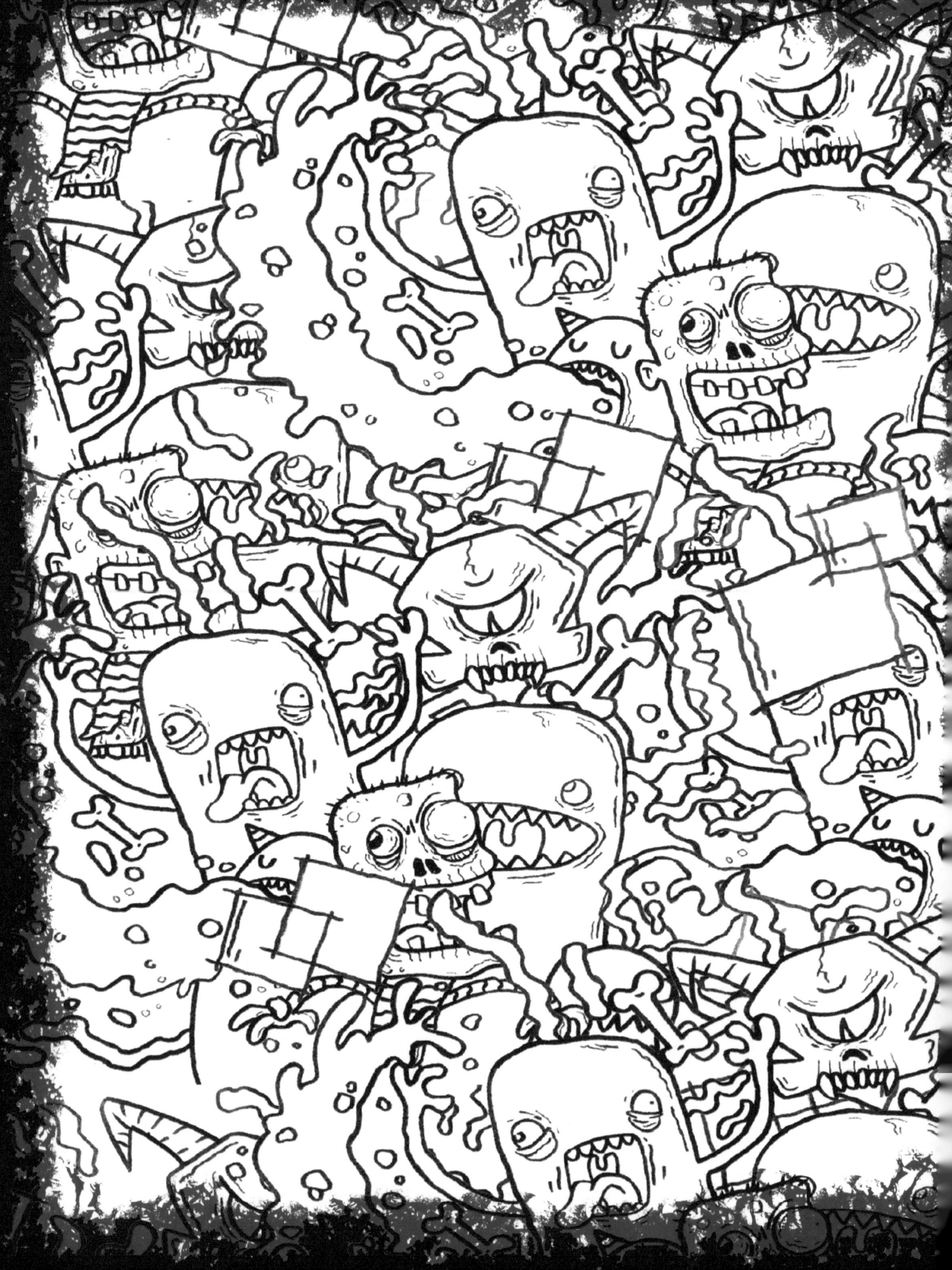

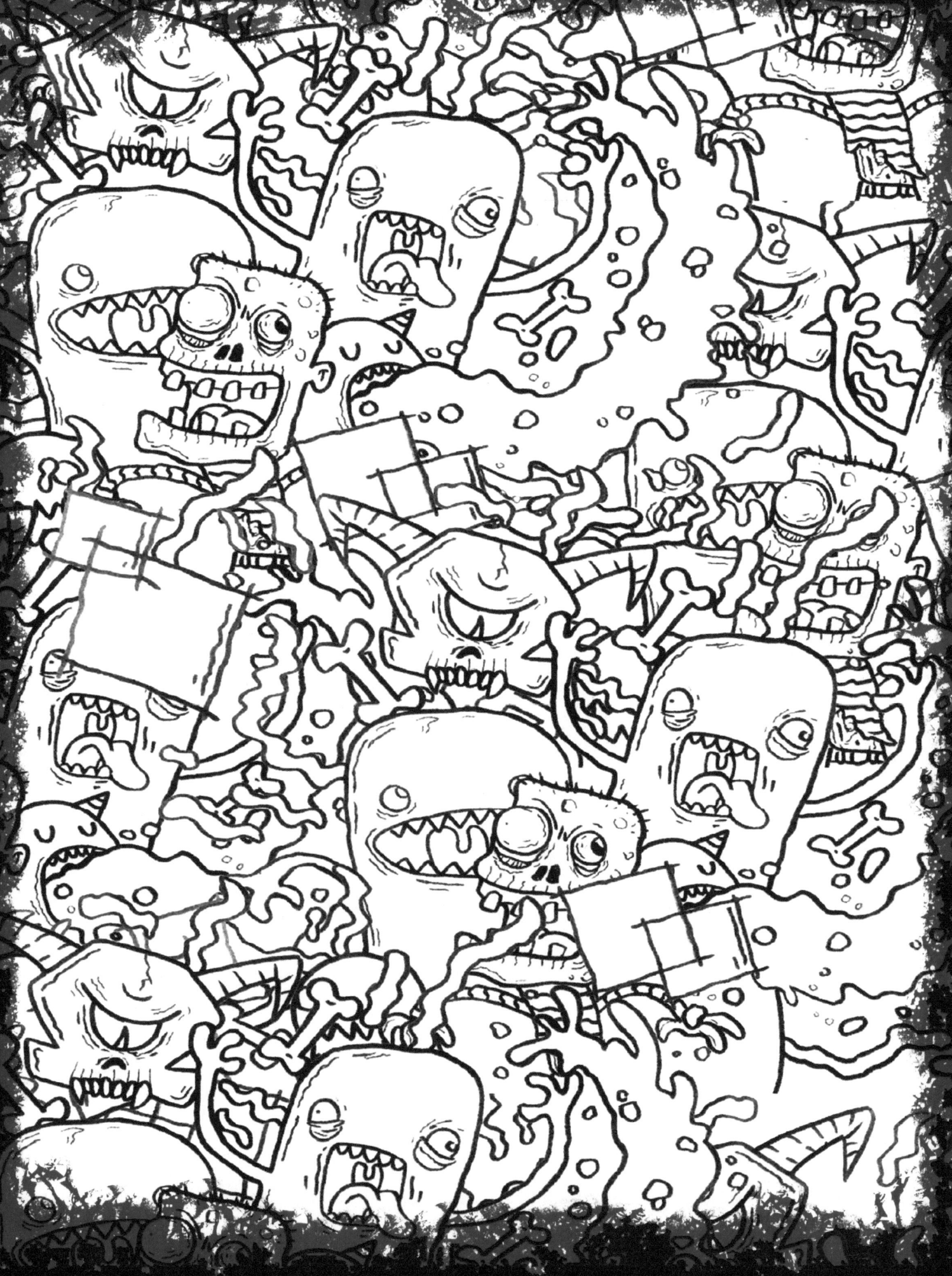

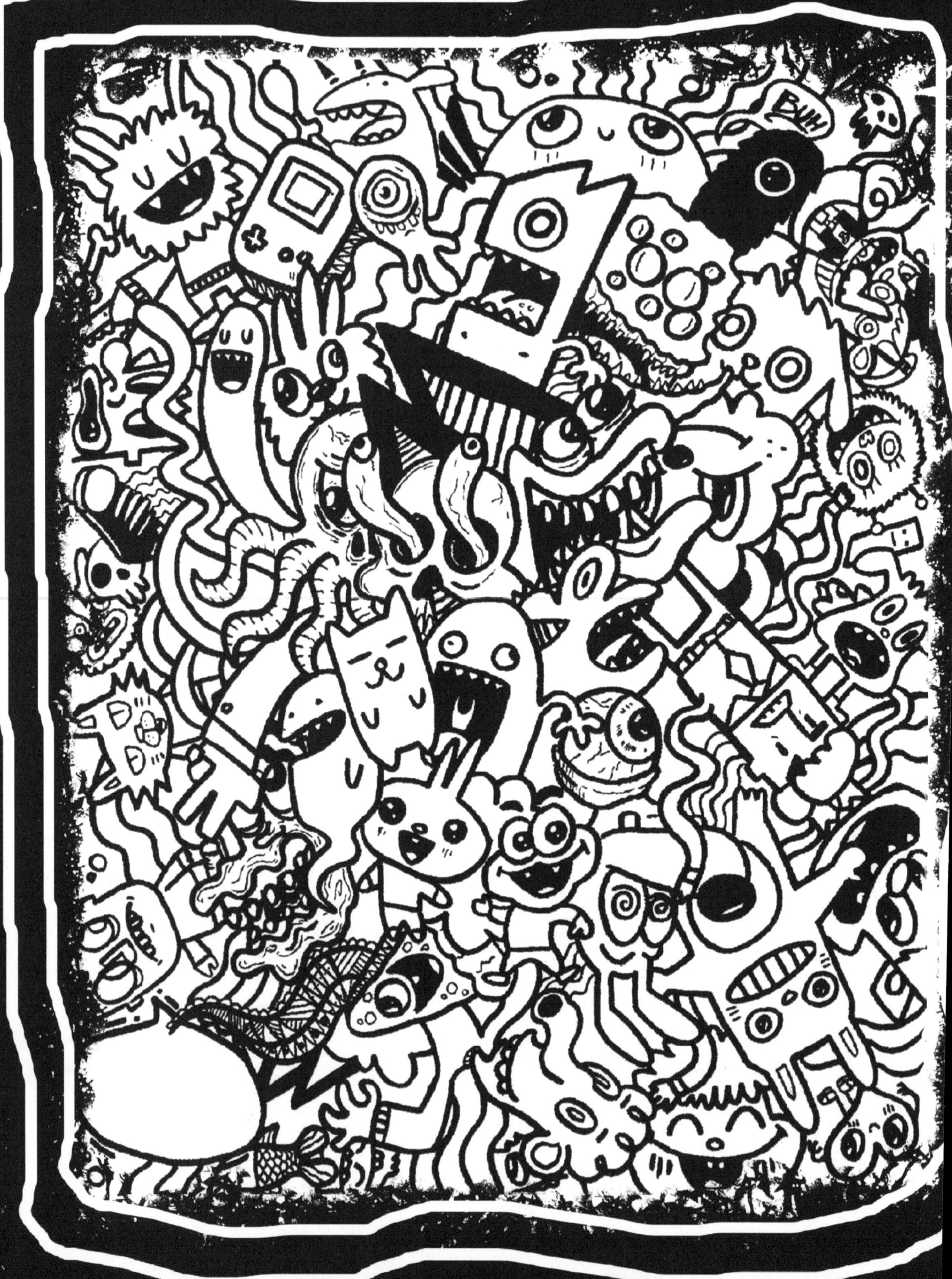

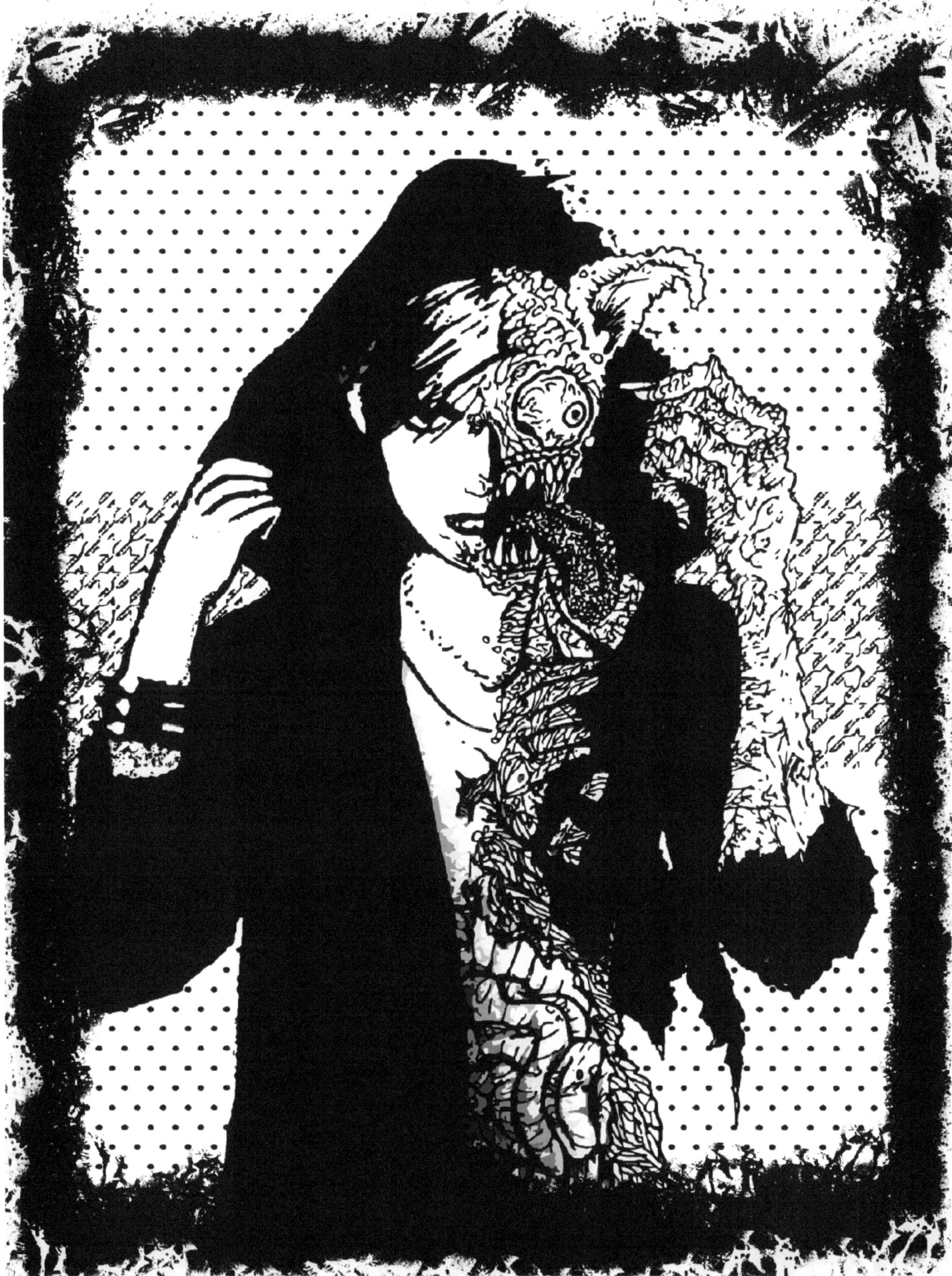

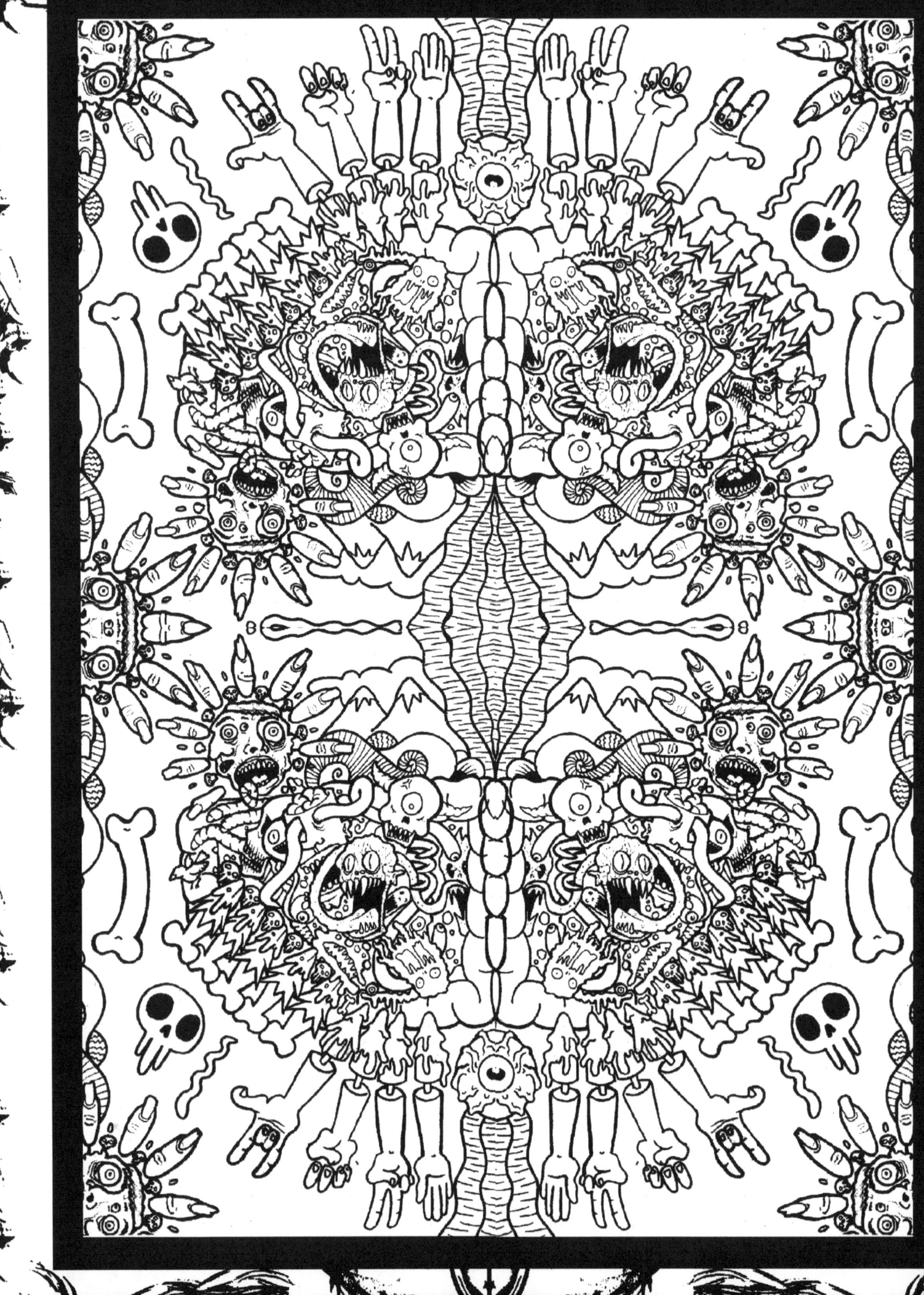

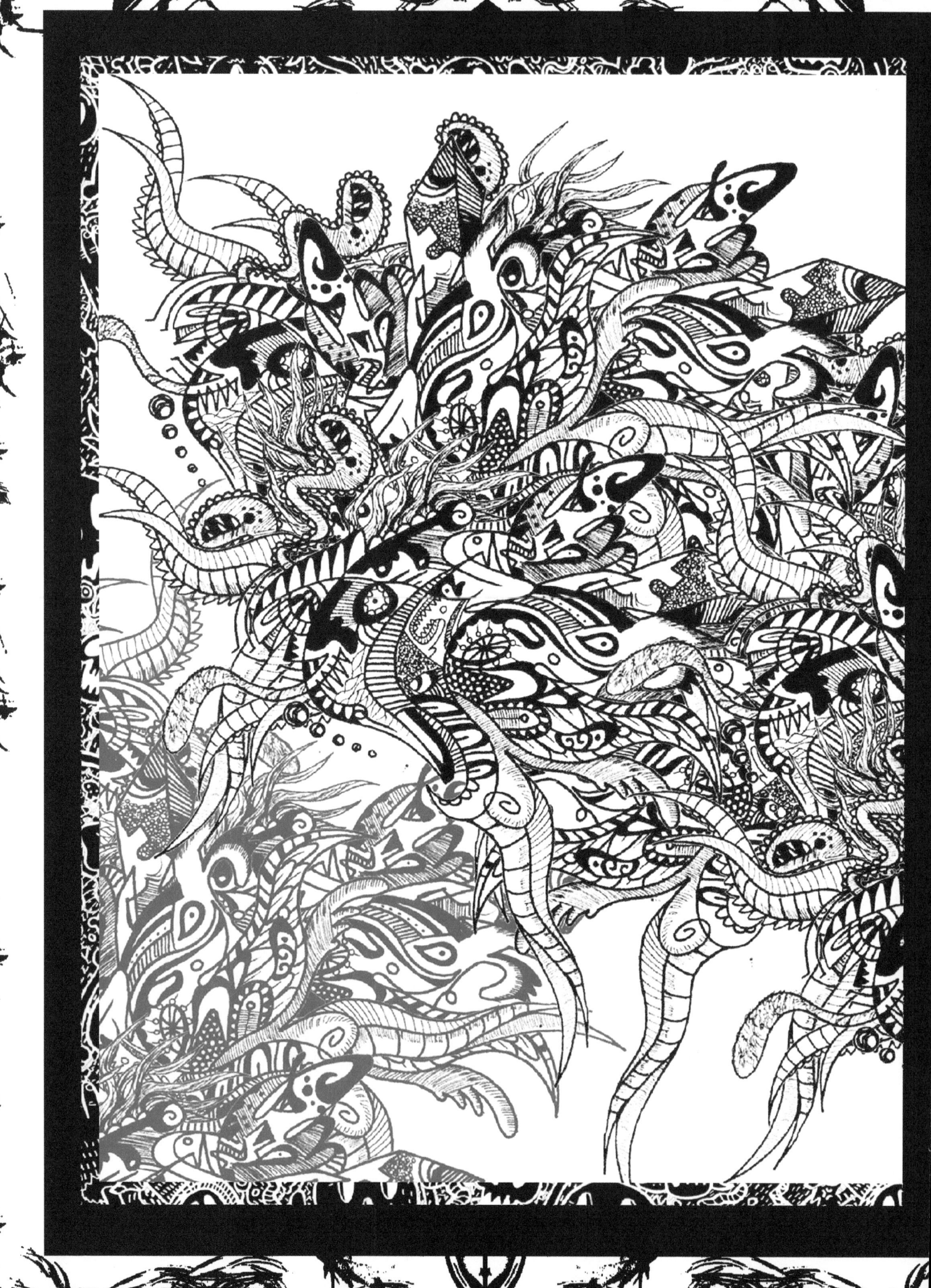

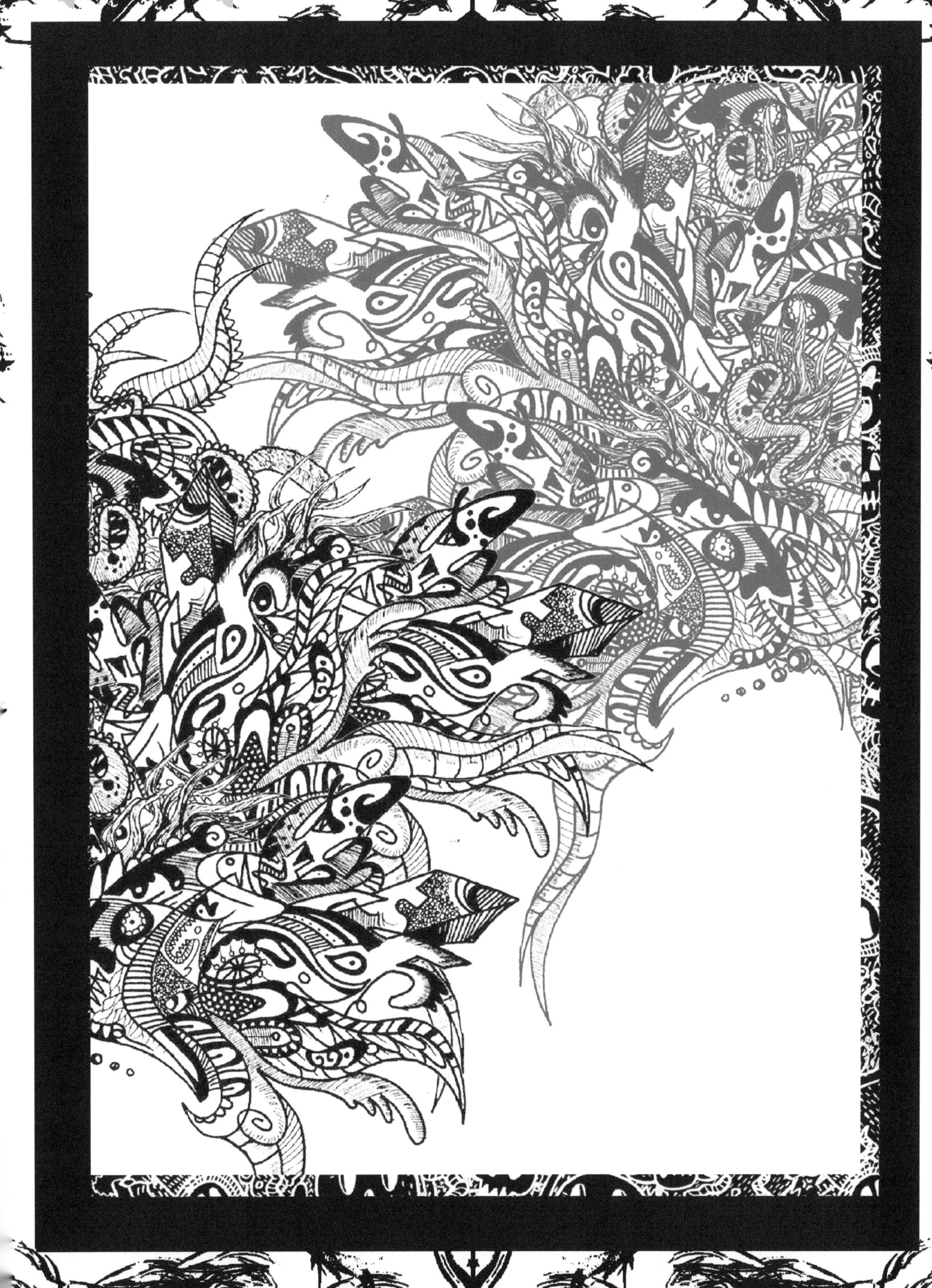

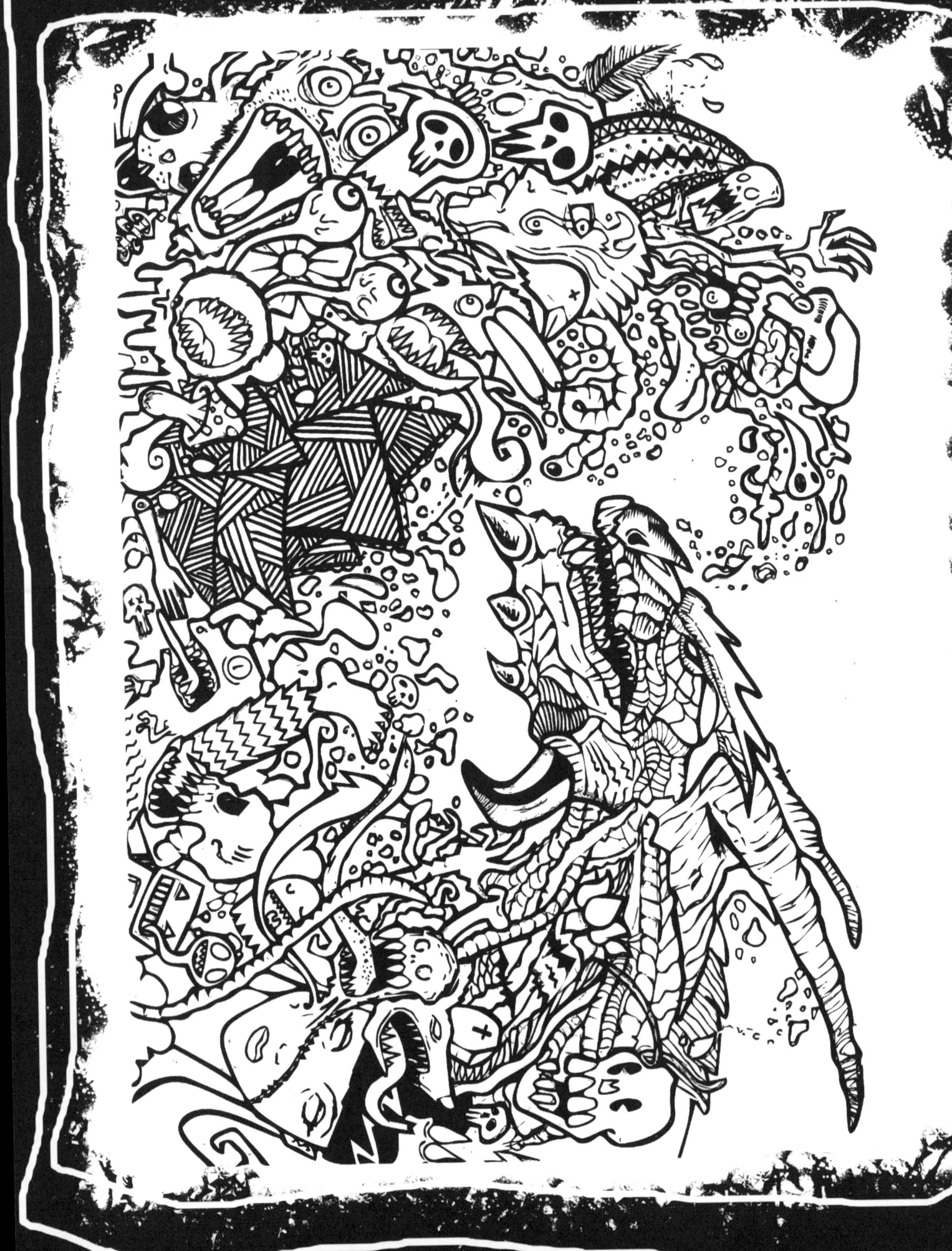

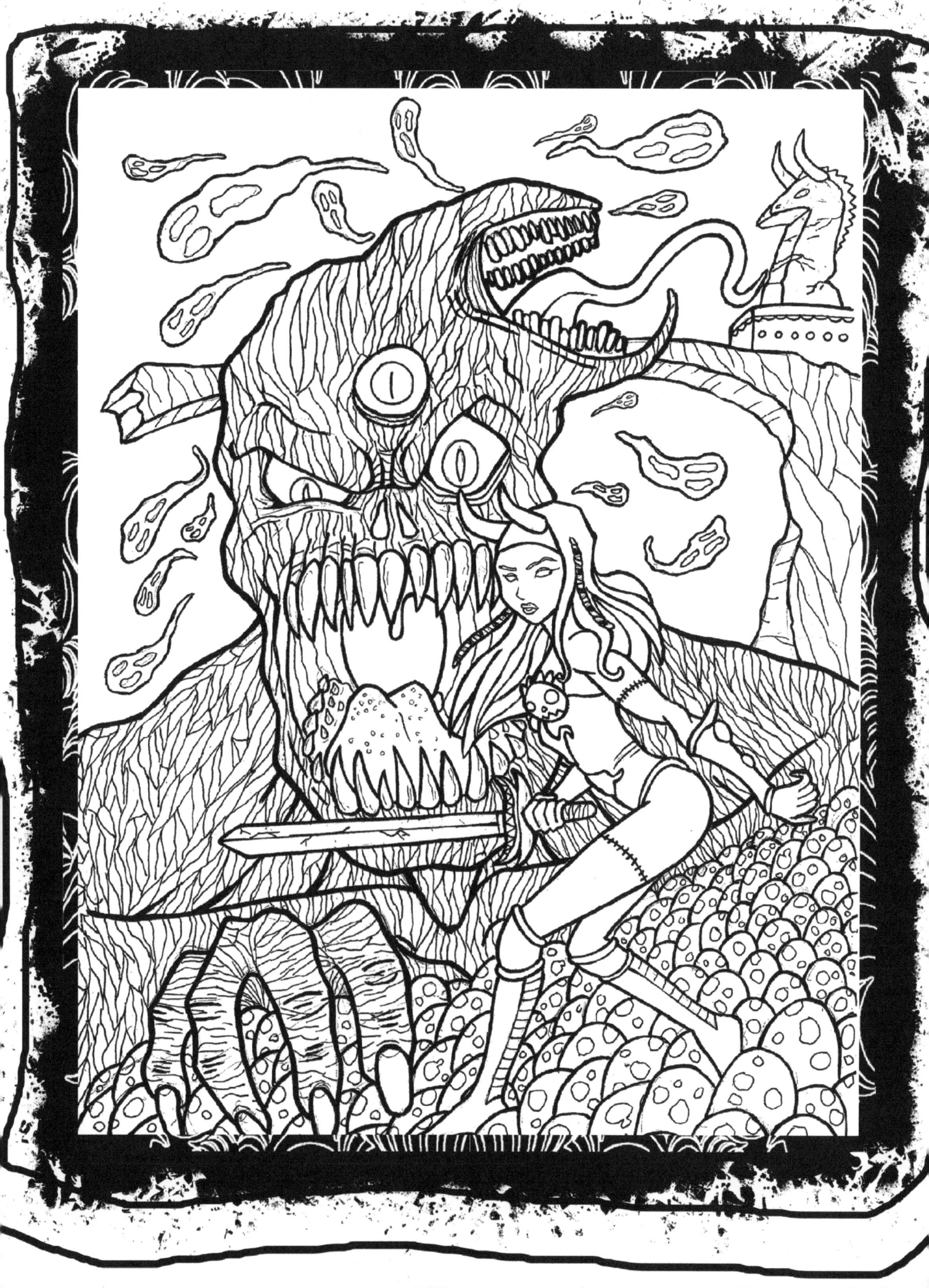

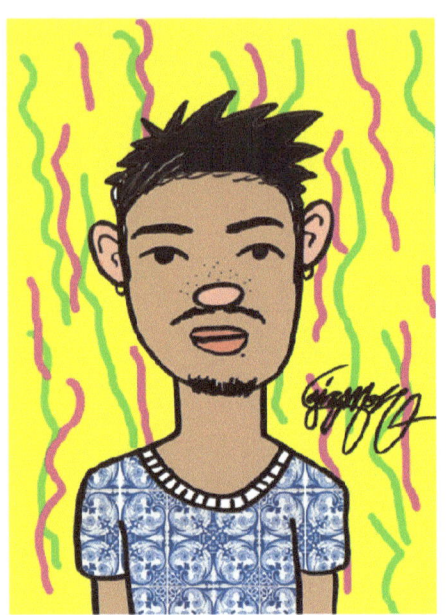

ABOUT THE ARTIST

Since he was a little boy, Gizmoh has fallen asleep with his head under a bookshelf full of comic and manga paperbacks, renaissance and surrealism compilations, stories, tales and epic novels. Surrounded by these book walls, a crowd of action figures closely stands by, waiting for a place on the first row, to take a look all around the room walls, covered with Gizmoh's original graffitis, stencils, stickers and vinyl pop-art.

But they know that not all Gizmoh's art is seen. Some nice part of it is just to be heard. Producing originals and remixes of different genres of electronic music has been keeping him seated in his red chair for hours since his 20's.

Gizmoh finds himself where he first got lost, somewhere in his boundless imagination.